Lives in Cricket: No

Jack Bond
Lancashire Lad, Lancashire Leader

Douglas Miller

First published in Great Britain by
Association of Cricket Statisticians and Historians
Cardiff CF11 9XR
© ACS, 2010

British Library Cataloguing-in-Publication Data.
A catalogue record for this book is available from the British Library.

ISBN: 978 1 905138 87 6
Typeset by Limlow Books

Contents

Introduction

Come down to Old Trafford at most times of year and observe the ground staff at work. There is a fair chance that you will find a small elderly figure patiently tending the practice pitches. As he moves at his own measured pace, there will be little to tell you that you are watching one of the iconic figures of Lancashire cricket. Nor will a perusal of statistics enlighten you: a career batting average of 25.90 with no one-day half-century and no pretence to bowl confirm that Jack Bond's career was that of a journeyman player. Only by digging deeper will you discover that he was a captain who restored the pride of a once great county at a time when its playing record had plumbed new depths of mediocrity.

It was at the launch of Simon Lister's book *Supercat*, a biography of Clive Lloyd, that I first came fully to recognise the respect with which his players still hold this true Lancastrian and devoted Methodist. Seeking signatures for the title pages of the new book, I approached a group of those who had played for the county with Clive. Jack Simmons and David Hughes happily signed, but both insisted that space must be left at the top of the page for the third member of their group, Jack Bond, the man under whom they had played more than 30 years earlier. So this was the esteem in which their former captain was still held!

Feeling sure Jack had a story to tell, I approached him in Sri Lanka and this short book has become possible through the many hours that he has spent with me, sharing memories of triumphs and of misfortunes, struggles and tragedy. It has been a privilege to hear his testimony and that of many of those who played alongside him. Nor should I forget Jack's wonderful wife, Florence, who made sure that he had sandwiches and cakes for two for our meetings at Old Trafford.

Whiteleaf, Buckinghamshire
March, 2010

Chapter One
'Don't call him Little John'

'Have you seen Little John?' Ruth Bond's two sisters would enquire.

'My mother got fed up of it,' Jack Bond now relates. '"I'm not having you calling him Little John – it's like something out of Robin Hood."' At his christening John David Bond had been given the first names of his father and of his maternal grandfather, but it was not long before the baptismal choice was causing confusion in the tightly-knit extended family. So, to avoid any spurious links with Sherwood Forest, it was decided that the future Lancashire cricketer should be called Jack.

Jack Bond was born on 6 May, 1932 'within a six hit of the local cricket club' at Nurse Berry's, Clamerclough House, Kearsley. Three days later his mother was allowed to take her baby home to the village of Little Hulton, three miles south of Bolton, where the Bonds owned a terraced house at 142 Worsley Road.

John Bond, a spinner in the thriving cotton industry, had married Ruth Lee, a weaver, in 1930 and Jack was to be their only child. 'But I never felt like an only child,' he now says. 'Two cousins lived next door and another cousin lived next door but one. We were virtually brought up as brothers and sisters in the war years, so I never felt the need of a brother or sister.'

At the centre of this little family group were Jack's maternal grandparents. His grandfather, David Grinrod Lee, was a master butcher whose business was at number 140 Worsley Road. Ruth's sister Maggie and family lived with her parents, while her other sister Annie resided at 138. A brother Jim lived in nearby Farnworth, also working as a butcher. David Lee died shortly before the outbreak of war and the three sisters then ran the shop until their brother was granted compassionate release from military service on account of his wife's poor health. When he returned, he took over the running of the Worsley Road business.

The Lee side of Jack's family were staunch Methodists, reflecting the childhood roots of his maternal grandmother. Grandma Lee, as

Jack always called her, had come to Lancashire to take up a position in domestic service at Worsley, but she had been born and raised in strong Calvinistic Methodist territory at Penmaenmawr on the North Wales coast.

Jack's paternal grandfather had been an engineer for Horrockses, a well-known spinning business, and this side of the family was Anglican. It was nevertheless through church activities that John and Ruth had met, but after their marriage in 1930 it was Methodism that would remain a defining influence in their lives.

Jack's parents, John and Ruth, in 1948, when John was chairman of Worsley Urban District Council.

A strong social conscience led John into local politics, where he remained active until a brain tumour brought about his death on the operating table in 1952, at the early age of 50. 'He was an old-fashioned Labour councillor,' Jack says. 'He was on the District Council for about fifteen years and nobody ever put up against him. That says something about the man, doesn't it?'

Soon after marriage, Jack's parents decided to convert the front room of their home into a fish-and-chip shop, his mother giving up her work at the mill to run the business. There is a natural sociability with Jack that has shaped his adult life, and this same family trait was a feature of life in the fish-and-chip shop. Moreover, John's position as a councillor meant that the Bond home was the first in the area to have a telephone. Soon the shop became akin to a phone booth: 'If anybody came into the shop requesting to use this telephone, there was no way, as the local fish-and-chip shop, that we could ever say no. And, of course, when people had to leave a number because they were in hospital and things like that, they'd give our number.'

There was another feature of living at the back of the fish-and-chip shop that Jack will never forget: 'We made the mistake of having a door bell put on the fish-and-chip shop door. People working in the mines on early shift used to be stood at the tram stop, and to shelter out of the rain they'd come up to the door and lean on the bell. That bell used to be going off at five o'clock in the morning.'

With his mother busy preparing the fish, Jack was often in the care of his grandmother, and it was she who regularly accompanied him to his first school. One day the pair came close to losing their lives. 'Just outside our house there was the tram line. It was a single line with a loop where the trams could pass. We crossed over the road – this is what they told me later in life – and we nearly died. As we crossed the road this tram came round the loop rather too quickly and jumped the rails and ended coming towards us.'

When war was declared, Jack was seven years old, still too young to appreciate its full consequences. He remembers the coal store behind the house being replaced by an Anderson shelter, but the family soon decided that they could provide themselves with better and more comfortable protection. 'The butcher's shop had a cellar where they used to hang the meat because they did their own killing. The cows would be driven from Manchester straight into the stalls where they would be killed. Then they would hang the meat. Well, when war came, they turned this cellar into an air raid shelter.' As far as Jack can recall, the nearest a German bomb came to Little Hulton was when the co-op at Kearsley was blown up; but Manchester was a more important target and, with plenty of false alarms, the three families would find themselves spending long hours huddled together in the cellar. 'The guns would be blasting off and the next morning we would be out picking up the shrapnel.'

'They were happy days!' Jack remembers. But for his father, working in the fire service in Liverpool, there were also moments of great danger that the young boy barely understood. 'He was in Liverpool when the blitz was on and in the middle of the morning he was walking down the street and he saw something stuck up in the road and this chap said, "Don't worry. It won't go off for another twelve hours." It was an unexploded bomb!'

* * * * *

From a young age sport played a big part in Jack's life. He had the ground of the Methodist Cricket Club, where his father played and served as secretary, only minutes from his home. Sadly, the ground was an early casualty of war, when it became the site of a warehouse for the storage of unprocessed rubber, the location chosen because of the drains that served the cricket field. But the war did not stop Jack enjoying cricket and football at his junior school, where he found a sport-loving headmaster, Jim Hardy, who played cricket for Walkden Moor Methodists in the local league, and who made competitive games of cricket and football an important priority for his young charges. Though he admits to neglecting the academic side of school life, Jack still made a favourable impression with Hardy, and the headmaster was influential in securing a place for him at Bolton School and persuading John Bond that his son would prosper there.

An independent fee-paying establishment, and one of the oldest schools in Lancashire, Bolton School can trace origins back to 1516, when records show it was 'a going concern'. The present school, with its Boys' and Girls' Divisions, came into being in 1913, when it was re-endowed by William Hesketh Lever, the soap manufacturer, soon to become the first Viscount Leverhulme, whose family had been involved with the school's welfare since the seventeenth century.

The Junior eleven at Bolton School, 1945.
Jack is next to the scorer in the back row.

Jack's own preference would have been to stay with his friends at the local secondary modern school instead of setting out each day on a two-bus journey to Bolton. But, for all the inconvenience of the travel, the new school brought its compensations, especially in sport. The master in charge of cricket was Ron Booth, a Yorkshireman, who quickly spotted that the pint-sized newcomer had a talent for the game. Jack won his Junior Eleven colours in 1945 and the next year he scored 66 in the Juniors' victory over Manchester Grammar School. There were then two years in the Second Eleven with a few appearances for the First Eleven in the second summer. Though his three innings in the first team brought just 26 runs, the *Boltonian* wrote of him as 'a natural cricketer who should be very successful in future years. He plays very stylishly and forcefully for his size and his catching and ground fielding are both first rate.'

Always one of the smallest members of the school sides he represented, Jack recalls one team photograph in which he had to stand on a house brick to reach the shoulders of his team-mates. But his size was no bar to winning his First Eleven colours in 1949, one of only five boys to do so. He took part in matches against other grammar schools as well as a few local club sides, and he particularly remembers that they also played Rossall, a well-known public school. 'They said we weren't good enough to play their first team. So we played the second team and generally gave them a good hammering!'

This year the *Boltonian* was able to record: 'His stroke play is a delight to watch and he excels against slow bowling.' However, Jack's overall batting record remained modest, 194 runs at 16.17, with a top score of 48 not out against R.J.Heslop's XI giving him third place in the averages. But, as in later life, it was his fielding that set him apart. 'I've still got a book that I was given for the fielding prize, a book with the school crest on it.' This prized possession bears a suitable inscription in the headmaster's writing: 'Allison Fielding Prize.

Jack's fielding was always prized, even in 1949.

F.R.Poskitt. 27.7.1949.' The presentation is fresh in Jack's mind. 'It felt nice shaking his hand after being whacked with the slipper for playing football when I shouldn't have been!'

If Jack's cricket prospered through going to Bolton School, he wonders if his reluctance to bother with the academic side of school life might have pegged him back in making a mark in the game. Had he gone on to university, as many of his contemporaries did, he feels he might have been noticed at an earlier age as a cricketer. Instead, Jack left school at the age of seventeen and his cricket was confined to playing at his local Walkden club, where he became a regular member of the second team until he was called up for National Service.

After leaving school, Jack's first employment was with the Lancashire Electric Power Company, where he worked in the personnel department, starting in the mailroom before moving on to looking after staff records. The company's main office was in Manchester and, as Jack understood it was about to re-locate to Bolton, it seemed a convenient place to work. But the move never took place during his time with the company.

'Are you courting?' Wilfred Pickles, a leading radio personality of the day, would invariably ask contestants on his popular quiz programme *'Have a Go'*. Had Jack Bond appeared, he could not have denied that he was losing his heart to a girl named Florence Fletcher, just a year younger than he was. Florence and Jack had known each other as young children, and they continued to meet at church socials and dances in their teenage years. Jack remembers 'a big old-fashioned band' that played in Moor Hall at Farnworth. 'The boys'd turn up and the girls'd turn up, then on Sunday afternoons we'd go for a walk on Market Street to the ice cream parlour. Lads of 15, 16, 17 – what else could you do?'

Jack recalls his first effort at taking matters a little further with Florence: 'I asked to take her to the pictures – to meet at the Ritz in Farnworth. And I didn't turn up! Because on Sundays my mum and dad always used to go to my grandmother's in Farnworth, and I hadn't asked permission to go and meet Florence.' Jack rang up later and all was forgiven. 'Then we were courting for a couple of years before I did my National Service.'

Like Jack, Florence was an only child. With a father Albert, who played for Farnworth Social Circle in the Bolton and District Association league, and a mother Annie who scored, cricket was bred into Florence from an early age. Jack relates a story of an unusual footnote to an absorbing game that took place at Adlington shortly after Florence's birth. 'After the match Albert and Annie got back to the bus stop and Albert said, "What have you done with Florence?" They'd left her in a carrycot at the cricket ground! She was only a month old. It must have been a hell of a match!'

In September 1950 Jack began his two-year stint as a National Serviceman, joining the Royal Army Pay Corps. His initial posting to Devizes was to be his last. After initial training, he moved to C Company, which was the overseas training wing and which was also responsible for training soldiers in other regiments who would eventually become Pay Corps sergeants when they returned to their own units. Commanding B Company was Captain Harry Thompson, later to rise to the rank of brigadier, who was captain of the station cricket side. Jack remembers him as 'a dour, out-and-out Yorkshireman', but his White Rose roots did not deter him from taking a paternal interest in the welfare of the newly arrived Lancastrian in one of the other companies. Thompson always kept an eye out for any new arrivals at Devizes with sporting talent, and he could see that in Jack he had a useful cricketer, who could also play table tennis and who would soon adapt to hockey.

Jack played regularly in the station cricket team alongside Thompson, who was a good medium-fast bowler, and he often accompanied Thompson to play for other sides. A friendship was forged that would last a lifetime. In the 1990s the pair were able to reunite at Southampton when a boundary fielder in a county match confirmed to the retired brigadier that it was indeed Jack Bond umpiring the match. Runs flowed from Jack's bat in the matches against local clubs and other military teams, and in his second season he was selected to represent the Royal Army Pay Corps against other branches of the Army. The highlight of his summer was the match against the Cross Arrows at Lord's.

Though Cross Arrows' matches have for many years taken place in late summer on the Nursery Ground, this match was played on the main ground, but the teams did not use the principal dressing rooms. Instead, they changed in the old professionals' quarters, now the Bowlers' Bar in the pavilion. Observing the traditions of an earlier age, they emerged onto the playing area from a side gate. Jack's opponents included several Middlesex players who had already made their mark in the first-class game or would soon do so. He mentions Jack Robertson, Syd Brown and Alan Thompson as batsmen, and there were two bowlers, Fred Titmus and Alan Moss, who would soon be playing for England, and another, John Warr, who had just done so.

Batting in the middle order, Jack came in shortly before the declaration, joining Harry Thompson at the wicket. He scored an undefeated 18, and he still remembers how the innings was composed: 'The first one was a six – it went over extra cover towards where the Warner Stand is now. That was a shot that, when I came to Lancashire, Stan Worthington tried to coach out of me – I had to keep the ball on the ground. Six, five, four, three and then we declared. The five was an overthrow.'

Jack's batting partner, still going strong at the age of 86, recalls that the six was off the bowling of Moss and he remembers the pace bowler's reaction: 'He said, "You can't do that to me." And Jack, in his broad Lancashire accent, said, "Can't I? Well I've just done it!"'

In years to come Lord's would become the ground on which Jack would enjoy many of the proudest moments of his career, but they would struggle to surpass the thrill of treading the hallowed turf for the first time – and joining a select band whose first scoring shot at Lord's was a six.

Over extra-cover.
The shot that Stan Worthington tried to discourage.

Chapter Two

'We thought you were nineteen'

Back in Lancashire for the 1953 season, Jack continued to play his cricket for Walkden, where he had been a junior member since his early teens. The Bolton League club's professional was a West Indian, Edwin St Hill. In a brief first-class career, six wickets for Trinidad against British Guiana had won him two Test caps as a first change pace bowler against the Hon F.S.G.Calthorpe's England side in 1929/30, and he was included in the West Indies party for the tour of Australia the following year. Though he enjoyed little success at the highest level, with just three expensive Test wickets, St Hill had been a prominent club cricketer in his native Trinidad, where he played for Shannon alongside his more famous brother Wilton.

Edwin St Hill had passed his fiftieth birthday when Jack played alongside him at Walkden, his experience of English conditions

Jack, captured by a Brownie camera at Walkden, 1953.

enriched by playing for Learie Constantine's XI and other teams in wartime matches that had taken him around Lancashire and given him a couple of appearances at Lord's. Now Jack recalls the elderly West Indian with obvious respect and affection: 'He was such a mild-mannered man, a real gentleman. He had time for everybody, time to talk and to listen. He was such a good bowler too. I admired his control, and it was from watching him that I first fell in love with the away swinger. Later on, as captain, I always liked to have an away-swing bowler.'

With Edwin St Hill's technical help and encouragement, Jack prospered, averaging 43 for the season. One match stands out in his memory, when he was picked to play against Westhoughton. In the opposing side was Eddie Paynter, the Lancashire left-hander of pre-war years, whose 20 Tests for England had brought him an average of 59.23. He secured a place in the game's folklore when he rose from a Brisbane sick bed to score 83 and steer England to an unlikely first-innings lead from which Douglas Jardine's men established their crucial 3 – 1 lead in the Bodyline series in 1932/33.

'I don't know whether he was their professional or whether he was playing for money in his boots,' Jack says, 'but he was fielding quite close in and we got talking after the match. He said, "I'll get you a trial at Old Trafford."' Jack heard nothing from the Lancashire club, and Paynter may not have followed up on his promise, but he had sown a seed. If Eddie Paynter thought he could bat, perhaps Jack ought to be seeking an opportunity to prove himself at a higher level.

The runs he had made at Walkden led to suggestions that he should try his luck at Radcliffe in the stronger Central Lancashire League. His Kearsley birthplace, being within the required five mile radius of Radcliffe, qualified Jack to join his new club. He realised that he might be thought ungrateful to those who had helped him through his youth cricket at Walkden. 'You're upsetting everyone,' he was told. 'You'll never make it,' some tried to persuade him. But despite the carrot of a pound a match to stay at Walkden, the six-pounds-a-week clerk decided to make the move.

'It was a lot of money in them days,' Jack now jokes, but it didn't dissuade him from making the move to a better league before it was too late. From the gentle Edwin St Hill, Jack now came under the wing of another man who was to prove a big influence on his development and remain a good friend in later life, Cec Pepper. One who has always listened to advice now found it coming in the ripe language of an Australian, who had played in the Victory Tests before settling in England to become one of the league's most successful professionals.

'It was the first time I came in touch with sledging,' Jack recalls. 'Some of his language was choice. We had a chap called Jeff Yates, a quick bowler from Little Lever. He was training to be a Congregationalist minister and he was in the team as well. It got to the stage where Cec would have to change in the toilet because of his language!'

Radcliffe made demands on those who expected first-team cricket. 'If you missed practice, you wouldn't get picked.' So twice a week, on Tuesdays and Thursdays, kit in hand, Jack would leave work and catch a train from Manchester to attend the practice nets at Radcliffe; and there was a bus journey home before he could sit down to a late evening meal. But life in the higher league had its compensations. 'One bonus was that, when we played away, the club hired a coach. That was really upmarket from Walkden, where you had to make your own way on the trams and buses. To be taken to the ground on a coach – you felt you were really going somewhere.'

Jack was soon in the runs and he was now performing on a stage where good performances would not go unnoticed. 'Then I had a real stroke of luck,' he remembers. In the 1950s Manchester boasted two evening papers, soon to be amalgamated, but then keen rivals, the *Evening Chronicle* and the *Manchester Evening News*. The *Chronicle's* cricket correspondent was Eric Todd, but the paper also took steps to involve itself with league cricket, sending a former Derbyshire player A.E.Lawton to cover matches and requiring him to find eight young players for whom the paper would fund winter coaching at Old Trafford.

Albert Edward Lawton, born in 1879, had made 131 appearances as an amateur for Derbyshire, leading the county at various times across eight different seasons before playing a handful of matches for Lancashire in the last three summers before the Great War. An old Rugbeian, well connected in the game, he had also played for W.G.Grace's London County. Now, in the twilight of his days, Lawton toured the principal league grounds of Lancashire, visiting a different club each Saturday, after which he wrote a substantial piece for publication in Monday's paper. At the top of his column ran the standard legend: 'Former Lancashire and Derbyshire player A.E.Lawton is on the look-out for young talent for special coaching to be paid for by the *Evening Chronicle.*'

In 1953 Lawton had been taken by the talent of a young Geoff Pullar at Werneth, and during the dismal summer of 1954, whenever rain did not frustrate him on his mission, he would pen the story of a match with particular and kindly emphasis on the performance of the younger players, sometimes offering wise observations on some of their shortcomings such as failure to back up properly when batting. The summer found him making notes of boys who would only reach their sixteenth birthday in mid-season, among them Alan Bolton, a pupil at Darwen Grammar School, who would soon be on the staff at Old Trafford, and Arthur Sutton, destined to become one of Cheshire's greatest players, a left-handed bat whom Lawton saw as 'a Jack Ikin of the future in the field.' Roy Collins, by now 20 and already employed at Old Trafford, was another to earn a mention, and there was a wistful reference to a son of Jack Iddon, a lad whose father might have captained Lancashire had he not been killed in a car crash shortly before the start of the 1946 season.

On Saturday 19 June, Lawton's chosen match was at Radcliffe, where the visitors were Crompton. Taking the chance to chat with both captains before the match, he learned first about the potential of five Crompton youngsters, most of them still in their teens. 'Next I tackled the Radcliffe captain, E.Ratcliffe, who told me they were not so well off for young players but he named John Bond as a 19-year-old "good 'un", who came to them this season from Walkden, where his batting average was 43.'

The outcome of the match, as so often in league encounters of the time, hinged on the performance of the two teams' respective professionals. 'Unfortunately this budding talent was up against Cecil Pepper and Sonny Ramadhin,' Lawton was later to report. Radcliffe, put in to bat, enjoyed a brisk start as Pepper hit a quick 32 before he was 'utterly deceived and bowled by Ramadhin', who finished with nine for 28 as the home side folded from 70 for five to 78 all out, only the captain among Pepper's team-mates reaching double figures. Crompton's batsmen also struggled, but 22 from Ramadhin settled the issue as his side got home with three wickets to spare.

Though Jack had imagined that the match in which Lawton had watched him must have been one in which he had prospered, it seems that this was the only occasion that the *Evening Chronicle* scout saw him in action. There is no record of how many Jack scored – he thinks it was seven, but his brief knock no doubt reinforced his skipper's high opinion, and he had put a marker down as one whose future scores should be noted. Whatever happened that day, Lawton left the ground with a false impression that was to play an important part in shaping the history of Lancashire cricket, for the '19-year-old' he had been watching was actually 22.

Most of those whose virtues were paraded each week in A.E.Lawton's column were teenagers or, at most, 20 or 21. Young Jack Bond, recalled as a fresh-faced youngster by those who first met him when he came to Old Trafford, may still have looked a borderline case when entering a pub, but in reality he had completed his National Service and within a year he would be a married man. As he drew up his list of eight to enjoy winter coaching at Old Trafford, would Lawton knowingly have included a young man of 22? We shall never know, but it seems unlikely.

His Peter Pan qualities intact, Jack would head each week for Lancashire's indoor school, a bleak and chilly shed, a coke stove in the corner providing its only warmth. 'Spending most of his time with his backside to this stove,' as Jack recalls him, was the county's left-arm spinner, Malcom Hilton, who had played four Test matches for England and who was now the winter assistant to the man who ruled supreme, Stanley Worthington, the county's head coach.

Stan Worthington was an imposing figure. Parading in the manner of a sergeant-major, he invariably sported a white cravat, which Jack remembers set off a face deeply sunburnt in both summer and winter. 'Whether it was a fake tan we shall never know,' Jack muses, 'but I don't remember him ever going abroad.' Reminiscent of the unpopular disciplinarian to be found on many a school's teaching staff, the head coach was a man whose unexpected appearance was always feared by the young professionals at Old Trafford.

A stalwart of Derbyshire, Worthington had played a major part in securing his county's only championship title in 1936. The same summer saw the only century he was to hit in his nine Test matches, against India at The Oval. It earned him a place in Gubby Allen's team to tour Australia that winter, but he was one of many disappointments and never played Test cricket after his return. Retiring from playing at the end of the 1947 season for a life as a coach, Worthington had taken over from the much-loved Harry Makepeace at Old Trafford. It was not the easiest succession.

'Harry was a great coach,' says Roy Tattersall, who joined the Lancashire ground staff in 1946. 'He could tell you what to do and how to do it. There'd be six or eight nets going on and someone would play a false stroke in the far net and he'd say, "What sort of a stroke do you think that was?" You thought he wasn't watching you, but he was watching all the nets.' Makepeace had taken the initiative and patiently helped the young Tattersall to convert from a journeyman seamer to an off-spinner whose bowling would win Test matches, imparting never-to-be-forgotten advice: 'Harry told me what to do and he emphasised that those three short legs, their lives depended on my bowling. He emphasised it so much that I realised it was essential to bowl a length – because their families were in my hands.'

The arrival of Stan Worthington brought a different coaching ethos to Old Trafford. To Roy Tattersall he was still an excellent technical coach, but 'he wasn't an easy person to get on with. You wouldn't ask him a lot of questions or anything like that.' To Frank Parr, wicket-keeper of the early fifties, who also knew both coaches, Worthington 'shouldn't have been allowed with young cricketers.' Devoting most of his time to the junior members of the staff, he could seem a curiously remote figure, often watching them from afar, as Roy Tattersall remembers: 'He'd get in Alan Wilson's car and sit in there and watch on his own for hours.' 'He always jumped into action when a committee member came along,' Frank Parr says with a chuckle.

A disciplinarian bringing pre-war values to the post-war age, Worthington was a stickler for smartness of dress, where he and the trombone-playing jazz musician Parr were destined to clash. Grammar school-educated and better-spoken than most of those who played alongside him, Parr was remembered by Roy Tattersall as 'doing *The Guardian* crossword and things like that, but he was a bit scruffy in his dress. Trousers would be a bit stained. He wasn't bothered if things didn't match.' Frank Parr has never been one for toeing the line, and this was to prove his downfall at the county club in an age of feudal relationships where, he recalls, 'in those days we weren't even allowed in the bar.'

Dress and table manners were both high on the agenda for Stan Worthington. Jack recalls the junior players being smarter turned out than the first team. 'He used to say, "Even if you can't play the game, you should look smart and look as if you can play." He didn't like scruffiness at all.' The old players laugh at recollections of Worthington at the tea table. 'If he saw anybody misbehaving he'd tell them in no uncertain terms,' says Roy Tattersall. '"You're having too many cakes and not letting anybody else have any!" He'd tell them off for stirring a cup of tea like this.' Taking a spoon to his cup of coffee, Roy vigorously rattled the sides of his cup to illustrate the forbidden method, and Jack later mimicked the genteelly raised fifth finger as the cup moved to the lips. The mickey-taking that bonds cricket teams thrives on such trivia, as Roy elaborates, 'They all started doing it in a funny way, Geoff Clayton and people like that.'

For all the fun that was always to be had at Worthington's expense, Jack grew to respect the coach's ability and methods. 'He was knowledgeable about the game, and he had the sense not to interfere too much with anybody's natural ability. I think that's the sign of a good coach. You've got to rely on your instincts in situations in a game, and Stan would allow people their natural ability until you did something absolutely wrong.'

For Jack, hitting over the top remained a challenge. Worthington advised him to cut the shot out, but as Jack's game, like that of most small men, was always based on back foot play and good timing, with less strength in the drive, hitting over extra cover had become an important part of his repertoire. He cut the shot out for a while, later bringing it in only when well set, 'but then I thought this is no good. Now the shot over the top is in every type of cricket I can think of.'

For all the youngsters offered a place on the winter coaching scheme there was the possibility of engagement on the county staff if they impressed the coaches. 'There were one or two who I thought were better than I was,' Jack says, particularly remembering a man named Jackie Hunter. 'But because of their jobs they couldn't afford to go into county cricket, whereas I was working as a clerk.'

Earning £6 or £7 a week at the power company, where he had now moved to the ordering department, a young man in Jack's position would better himself financially, during the summer months at least, if he were taken on by Lancashire, one of the more generous of the county clubs. So when the sub-committee recorded of J.D. Bond that he was 'to be offered engagement at a weekly wage of £10 until the end of the cricket season,' there was little to prevent Jack from accepting – except the little matter of his honeymoon.

Jack and Florence on their wedding day in 1955.

Worsley Road North Methodist Church,
as it was when Jack and Florence were married.

Jack and Florence had married on 2 April 1955 and they had departed for one week's holiday. 'We went to Jersey, which was quite something in those days. When we got back, a letter had arrived. We were away a week and the letter had arrived just as we left. So there it was waiting for me saying, would I go and see Geoffrey Howard, the Secretary at Old Trafford, on a certain day. And it was a day while we were away on our honeymoon. So I thought the chance had gone!'

Jack need not have worried. By the standard of others offered the possibility of a contract, his initial lack of response had not been an exceptional misdemeanour. The club's minutes record that the schoolboy Alan Bolton had not replied and that, as there had been the same apparent lack of interest from N.H.Cooke, 'a further letter should be sent to him in a registered envelope.'

Reassured to find that Geoffrey Howard was still keen to see him, Jack presented himself at Old Trafford. Like most first-time employees, he was faced with all manner of forms to complete. His date of birth was required. 'I wrote six, five, thirty two.' Geoffrey Howard's face dropped. 'We thought you were 19,' he said. By this time Jack was almost 23. Ignorance or a slip of the tongue by the Radcliffe captain the previous summer and the unquestioning acceptance of Jack's age by A.E.Lawton had taken him to the brink of a contract that might never have been on offer to a man of his advanced years. 'With all the publicity, by this time they couldn't really have it put in the papers that I was too old. I felt I was quite lucky really to be taken onto the staff.'

Jack pays tribute to the integrity of Geoffrey Howard in this awkward situation: 'He was such a lovely man, a very honest and genuine man. And once an offer had been made, because they had made mistakes in not checking it all out, he just let it go through.' Throughout the ups and downs of the next ten years, Geoffrey Howard would remain a sometimes lone voice of sanity and humanity amid committee and dressing-room disharmony. From 1956 he would have at his side as his personal secretary Rose FitzGibbon, 'a mother figure' in Jack's eyes and a wonderful servant of Lancashire, who was destined to become the first female secretary of a county club.

Chapter Three
'You're a professional cricketer now'

Hornby and Barlow, Archie MacLaren, the Tyldesleys, Harry Makepeace, George Duckworth, Eddie Paynter ... when Jack signed his contract he was joining a club proud of its traditions and its successes on the field. Always a county to be reckoned with, Lancashire's golden era had come in the inter-war years when, in the five summers from 1926 to 1930, there were four championship titles and one second place. Then, in 1934, had come another Championship.

When the War brought a halt to county cricket, Lancashire had only twice fallen as low as eleventh in the table, their average position across 46 seasons from 1890 a shade better than fourth. Ten years after the war, memories of the glory days were still fresh in the minds of supporters of middle age or older. And they waited with growing impatience for the county to take the crown once more. There had been near misses. Jack Fallows, pitchforked into the captaincy in 1946, led the county to third place as did Ken Cranston the following summer. In 1950 Nigel Howard's side shared the title with Surrey, and on three other occasions during his time in charge, Lancashire finished third. But second or third place in the table was not the members' idea of a satisfactory season.

Owners of an historic Test match ground and with a healthy membership, even at a time when budgets were being trimmed, Lancashire was in all respects a big county. The club boasted a large and comparatively well-paid playing staff and, at a time when most of the smaller brethren were worried about the viability of running a second team in the Minor Counties Championship, Lancashire's programme was for 20 matches, more than any other county chose to play.

With such a large staff, there was a hierarchy that newcomers quickly learned to understand. Capped players occupied the main upstairs dressing room with its balcony overlooking the ground, while the juniors piled into their own less well appointed room

'You're a professional now.'
Jack on the Old Trafford practice ground, in 1955.

below with a huge sash window that had to be hauled up to let in the light. 'We called it "The Dogs' Home". You never ventured upstairs, and you didn't speak to anyone unless you were spoken to.' For net practice the juniors were expected to reach the ground well before the capped players put in an appearance, and they would do a disproportionate share of the bowling. 'One or two of the seniors did treat you as though you were servants,' Jack remembers. 'They'd go out with their pads on, not intending to take part in the bowling. I never saw Cyril Washbrook bowl a ball in the nets, probably Winston Place the same.'

For the young professionals, there were occasional twelfth-man duties as well being 'on the dollies', or 'OTD' as it would appear on team sheets to indicate the two players who had been assigned to help man the score box. And they spent long hours bowling at members who had booked net practice. 'They'd ring up Stan Worthington and book an hour's net and you'd have to bowl at them. They'd put sixpence or a shilling on their stumps, but they didn't just defend their stumps with the bat, they defended them with their pads as well. You probably ended up with 50 lbws but not a penny in your pocket!'

Jack was chosen for the Second Eleven's first match, against Warwickshire on the GEC Ground at Coventry, which began on 18 May 1955. With two of the side's most regular players, batsman Sid Smith and leg-spinner Tommy Greenhough having a run in the first team, the chosen side, in batting order, read: P.Barcroft, K.Bowling, G.Pullar, J.D.Bond, R.Collins, M.G.Rhodes (captain), G.Blight, F.D.Parr, J.Wood, F.Goodwin, F.Moore.

Peter Barcroft, Ken Bowling and Gerry Blight, as batsmen, and leg-break bowler Jim Wood were four of the many young cricketers who were retained on the staff for a few seasons without breaking into the first-class game, but Geoff Pullar, still an amateur, was destined for Test cricket, while Roy Collins, who was to become a good friend of Jack's, would also win his county cap. Frank Parr, once highly rated as a wicket-keeper, had been displaced from the senior team the previous summer, while Fred Goodwin, a Manchester United half-back, and Freddie Moore were two quick bowlers taken onto the staff in the quest to find an opening partner for Brian Statham.

Captaining the side was Michael Rhodes, an amateur with some pretensions to being a batsman. 'He was an ex-military man. His father was a former chairman of the club. He led the second eleven as if it was a military operation. He tried to instil a vast amount of discipline in people, but a number of the older players didn't take a lot of notice of him.'

It was Parr with whom Jack shared a room at the hotel. 'He was virtually looking after me and when we went down to dinner he ordered trout. I don't think I'd ever had trout in my life, and it was the most expensive meal that he could order. The club were obviously paying for it, and it was because he was under a bit of a cloud and felt he should have been in the first team. I said, "Frank, what are you doing?" He said, "Well, I might as well make the most of it. I don't know how long I'm going to be here!" I'll never forget that.'

Jack made a solid start to a season in which he was to play in 19 of the 20 matches. Second top scorer in the first innings, with 44, he followed with an undefeated 23, the only knock of any substance in setting a declaration target. Then, in the next match, he played a lone hand for 37 in a second innings total of 77 against Surrey at Old Trafford. When he made 71 against Derbyshire at Old Trafford, it was his first half-century for a county side, and towards the end of July he passed three figures for the first time, making 107 not out against Surrey Second Eleven at Beddington Park. With high scoring always difficult in the two-day matches, Jack's 735 championship runs were the team's highest individual aggregate, while his average of 29.40 was comfortably above most of the other specialist batsmen.

Jack's century was timely. It came just a week before Surrey's first team, champions for the previous three years, were due at Old Trafford; so, when Geoff Edrich suffered a lapse in form, it was to Jack that the selectors turned as his replacement. 'With me being 23 they probably thought we'd better have a look at him at the first opportunity to make a decision about me at the end of the season,' he says. But his promotion was merited. The other batsmen in the second team – Barcroft, Bowling, Smith and Pullar – were all below him in the averages, and he always added keenness to the fielding.

Jack could hardly have asked for a tougher introduction to first-class cricket. The visitors' principal bowlers – Alec Bedser, Peter Loader, Jim Laker and Tony Lock – were all current or recent choices for England, and that year they would ensure that no

Surrey match was left drawn. Has there been an attack of greater potency in the annals of county cricket?

Batting first, Lancashire began well. There was 109 from Jack Ikin, and it was not until midway through the final session that the third wicket fell with the score on 218. That summer, Lock would take 149 wickets at 12.34 in the Championship. He was bowling when Jack came in – from the downstairs dressing room, where he kept his kit. He remembers a good crowd, perhaps 15,000, to see the champion county. 'Obviously I was quite apprehensive, but when I was walking to the wicket Peter May said, "Good afternoon, Jack." It's always stuck in my mind, more shock than anything. I'd never met him before, only seen pictures of him as England captain. A perfect gentleman, apparently he always found out if there was a new player he hadn't met. Then there was all the build-up in the papers – they were talking of me as another Winston Place. I think I suffered from a bit of shell shock.'

His innings lasted only a few balls: Bond, J.D. c Stewart b Lock 0. 'It seemed a long way out, but it seemed a lot longer coming back when I'd got a duck.' In 4.1 overs Lock took six wickets to end with eight for 82 as Lancashire were all out for 248. There was a catch for Jack off Roy Tattersall as Surrey conceded a 30-run lead. Then their bowlers got to work again. This time Lock and Laker shared the spoils as Lancashire could manage only 125, with Jack scoring just one before offering a return catch to Lock. The Surrey batsmen then cruised to a seven-wicket win.

An unchanged team was named for the weekend visit of Glamorgan. 'I'd just met Stuart Surridge and my second match was against Glamorgan with Wilf Wooller. Quite a baptism!' Once again Ikin was in fine form with 107 and Cyril Washbrook was on his way to 131 when Jack joined him at 257 for four. The pair added 72 in good time, Jack's 25 helping to an overnight declaration at 362 for nine. Glamorgan batted slowly throughout Monday, and on Tuesday it rained, so Jack's sortie into first-class cricket ended in anti-climax – apart from his pay packet. His £10 a week salary was always topped up by £1 if he played a minor county game, but he well remembers the difference two first team matches made as he counted what was in his envelope. 'I think I got £29 that week!'

His first county season behind him, Jack turned to his other great love – football. He resumed playing as a wing half for his Methodist club in the local league. 'People from that league had gone on to play for Bolton Wanderers. It was a reasonable standard.' But his football was short-lived. Around this time Florence was expecting their first child, and she felt that Jack should face up to his family responsibilities and stop playing. 'She said, "You're a professional cricketer now. If you break your leg or get injured, that's the end of that."' Rather reluctantly Jack obeyed and promptly burnt his boots. The following week a neighbour passed him a message. 'He said, "You'll never believe this, but a fellow from Wolverhampton Wanderers came looking for you last Saturday. I told him you'd stopped playing and burnt your boots!'

No longer an active player, Jack became an avid follower of Bolton Wanderers. With Florence and her father Albert in an Ariel sidecar, he would mount his BSA 600 side-valve motor bike and together they would ride up and down the country. 'We always used to take two big blocks of wood to stand on. Not only did they make us higher than other people, but the concrete floors weren't as cold when you were stood on the terraces.' An industrial injury to Albert around 1960 brought some financial compensation and the family used the money to upgrade from the motor bike to their first car.

In later years Jack would retain his passion for football, but as the fortunes of Bolton waned so he found a new team to support. His allegiance to Liverpool came about through getting to know Bob Paisley in the days before he succeeded Bill Shankly as the club's manager. 'Whenever Lancashire played at Aigburth and anyone was injured, Bob would come over and treat the lad. He was the physio – well he was a rubber really, but that's what he called himself.' The friendship blossomed and, when Jack became captain of Lancashire, the youngster who had stood on the wooden blocks was able to take a comfortable seat in the directors' box.

The main winter sport in which Jack participated was table tennis, a game he had first come across at the Methodist church. In his early teens he had gone down to watch the men's matches. When the players took a break for a cup of tea and a plate of potato pie, Jack and other youngsters would take over the table. 'It got to the stage where I was getting better than some of the men,' he says, and soon he was playing for the men's team on merit. In later life he played for Market Street Table Tennis Club in the Farnworth League and reached inter-league standard.

There were no first-team bonus payments for Jack in his second summer with Lancashire, when his Second Eleven figures – 494 runs at 23.52 – did not quite match his debut season, but it was enough for his contract to be extended. In 1957 his season began with 181 against Northumberland, and a further run of good scores – 102 against Notts, a pair of fifties against Cheshire and another half-century against Yorkshire – won him a place in the first team. The senior side had started the season brightly, but three defeats in four matches had prompted changes. With macabre timing it meant that Jack would once again be playing against Surrey at Old Trafford.

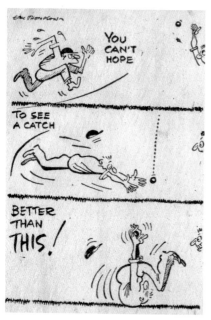

How Eric 'Sketchbook' Thompson of the Daily Mail saw Jack's catch in the home match against Surrey in June 1957.

This time Lancashire spent the first day in the field – and Jack made his mark with a catch off Tattersall that found the newspapers searching for new superlatives. For one reporter it was 'the catch of the year'; for another, 'the catch which Old Trafford venerables say was the greatest they have ever seen.' Peter May, at his imperious best, had reached exactly 100 when 'Bond raced 50 yards from long-off, launched himself seven yards into space, got both hands to the searing ball, rolled over twice – and triumphantly held it up.' Jack reads the old report with some astonishment 'Fifty yards! And diving seven yards – Superman couldn't have done that!' The grateful bowler remembers his own disbelief and adds: 'He was a very good fielder, was Jack. Close to the wicket, too, he made some beautiful catches.'

In an innings defeat, with most batsmen failing and not a first-innings run coming from the last six batsmen, Jack, at number six, scored nine as he 'tackled Lock bravely' and 12, his second dismissal ending the match when Lock took a fine return catch. Retained in the side for the rest of the season, Jack was in the runs against Cambridge University with 53 and 59 as Lancashire slumped to another innings defeat after the university batsmen had tucked into a second-string attack. A loss to Leicestershire had extended Lancashire's bad trot – six defeats in eight matches – when Somerset came to Old Trafford. The team's fortunes now turned round. Paving the way to an innings victory was a hard-hitting 72 from Jack, in which he went to his fifty in 'majestic manner' as he straight drove Jack McMahon for six. With an innings that 'put heart into the county at the right moment', he dominated a ninth-wicket stand of 69 with Tattersall, to which the off-spinner contributed just ten. This was to be Jack's highest score of a season that brought him three more championship fifties and 608 first-class runs at 19.61.

Jack had come into the side at a time of change. When he arrived at Old Trafford two years earlier, there had been a settled batting line-up. For the best part of a decade the runs had come from names schoolboy supporters could rattle off: Washbrook, Place, Ikin, Edrich, Grieves and Wharton. The first crack appeared in that first summer of 1955, when Winston Place started the season with a string of poor scores and was dropped, never to return. Playing alongside him in the second team, Jack soon learned to understand why Place was such a well-liked cricketer and remains grateful for tips he was able to pass on. A vague attempt to install Place as assistant coach did not come to fruition and tears ran down his face when his contract was not renewed at the end of the season.

There were others among the senior players to whom Jack would turn for help and advice as he struggled to make his mark in the first-class game. 'Geoff Edrich, he was a great influence, he was like a father to me. And John Ikin was another fatherly figure; he would look after the youngsters on the field.' The long-serving wicket-keeper Alan Wilson was another ready to help a newcomer, while the one who looked after the players' rights was Alan Wharton. 'He was the one you'd go to if you wanted to make a point to the captain or committee. He knew a lot about the workings of the club and the people in charge.'

Roy Tattersall was one who particularly befriended Jack. Coming from Bolton, he offered regular lifts into Old Trafford in his

Cortina. 'Not everyone had a car in those days,' Jack points out. 'I knew of his background in the Bolton league and he knew of mine.' Tattersall's league career had started before the war, his first game, for Bradshaw before he moved to Tonge, coming as it has for so many: 'I got this job putting the score up. A pound a year I got – ten shillings in June and ten shillings in September. I was eleven or twelve. One day they were short. Someone didn't turn up and they asked me to play.'

The one man towards whom Jack felt no warmth was his captain Cyril Washbrook, who had taken over from Nigel Howard in 1954. One of the county's greatest batsmen, Washbrook was a man Jack found rather aloof with his interest focussed on those he felt had England potential rather than the lesser players. 'I felt I needed all the help I could get, but I didn't get it from Cyril.' Jack was not alone in finding Washbrook a difficult leader. Frank Parr had made his mark as a crowd-pleasing wicket-keeper who would dive around in spectacular fashion – he is a great admirer of Geraint Jones among modern keepers, and in 1953, when he had just been capped, MCC made enquiries about the possibility that he might tour the West Indies as reserve to Godfrey Evans. Under Washbrook's captaincy, and well aware that his lifestyle as a jazz musician did not meet with the approval of a skipper he now describes as 'making Genghis Khan look like a liberal', Parr played only five more matches before his career as a first-class cricketer was over. Cricket's loss was to become jazz music's gain: some years later Frank Parr would become the manager of Acker Bilk.

Roy Tattersall is another with reason to resent the way he was handled by his county skipper. An experienced and thinking Test-match bowler, whose principal weapons were variations of pace and angle of attack – rather than power of spin – he had found Nigel Howard a sympathetic captain; but 'Washbrook wanted people to bow and scrape to him. He sometimes *told* me how to bowl. "Go round the wicket" or "Go over the wicket". Nigel was good – he understood me. But with Cyril you had to do what he said. He didn't get the best out of me.'

On his improbable route to the captaincy of Lancashire, Jack would take note of the strengths and weaknesses of those under whom he played. With Washbrook, he felt that too often games were allowed to drift, and yet his overbearing manner still kept junior players on their toes. 'He fielded at cover and I was extra cover and I had to do all the chasing. And he ran me out a few times. If Washy said "Run", you ran!'

With five wicket-keepers at one time on the staff, Jack remembers the seasons when Jack Jordan was first choice. 'He was from Burnley, an excellent wicket-keeper, and he used to be stood up close to the stumps and, just as the bowler was coming up to bowl, you could see his eyes – they wouldn't be looking where the ball should be coming from. He'd be glancing at Cyril. What he was expecting I don't know, but he hardly took his eyes off Cyril. Whether he lived in fear of him, I don't know – some people certainly did!'

Man management, at which Jack would later excel, was an alien concept to Washbrook. In 1956 Roy Tattersall was challenging Glamorgan's Don Shepherd in the race to 100 first-class wickets. Both were in the nineties – then Roy was dropped. 'We had a match at Liverpool. They put a team sheet up and my name wasn't on it. I said to Stan Worthington, "Can you tell me why I'm not playing tomorrow?" He said, "Ours is not to reason why. Ours is but to do and die." I was dumbfounded – I'd taken most wickets in the country. He said, "I can't explain it to you."'

Left out for eight matches, Roy found hurtful rumours circulating that he had been misbehaving, rumours that led to a minute-book entry that he had been omitted 'simply because he was temporarily out of form and the sub-committee felt that, in omitting him and playing another in his place, they were strengthening the side.' A word from Washbrook might have been expected, but none was forthcoming. 'You couldn't consult anybody,' Roy says. 'Even with the captain you had to be very careful what you said, because obviously you were hoping for a benefit.'

The years of Washbrook's captaincy coincided with continuing disappointment in the Championship: tenth, ninth, second, sixth, seventh, fifth. Second place in 1956 owed much to Geoff Edrich, who had deputised as captain in ten matches and managed to lead the side to six of its twelve victories. This was also a time of continuing transition in the batting line-up. After his successful captaincy in 1956, Edrich moved on to devote his leadership skills to the Second Eleven. At the end of the following summer Ikin, injured for most of 1956, retired. By now a place had been found for Jack Dyson, who never quite fulfilled Washbrook's high hopes for him. From 1956 Geoff Pullar had become a regular, to be joined two years later by Peter Marner, whose progress had been hampered by a rugby injury, and by Bob Barber, whose time at Cambridge had ended. For Jack – as for Roy Collins, Brian Booth and others – there would be years of scrapping on the fringes for a place.

Chapter Four
'After all, it's only a friendly match'

Though the selectors retained faith in Jack, picking him for all the early matches in 1958, he endured a summer as bitterly disappointing as the weather. Where championship runs in the modern game average around the mid-thirties, the summer of 1958 saw them coming at no more than 21.13. Jack's own first-class tally was just 133 at 9.50, though once he had returned to the second eleven he became one of the most prolific batsmen in a side Geoff Edrich led to fourth place in a Minor Counties table of 32 teams.

In the baking summer of 1959 runs flowed more freely. This time Jack started in the second team, biding his time for an opportunity. A century against Northants in the new Second Eleven Championship, followed by 78 in the return fixture, earned him a call when the Indians came to Old Trafford. An undefeated 66, albeit in a total of 400 for five, made it hard for him to be dropped. A month later came his first championship century, against Nottinghamshire at Trent Bridge. Having already top-scored with 76 in the first innings, his best first-class score to date, he went one better in his second knock when acting captain Alan Wharton promoted him to number three and allowed the innings to run until he had passed three figures. 'I was always grateful to Alan for sending me in at number three and giving me my chance. He knew how much it would mean to me, as an inexperienced, uncapped player.'

Sadly, with Statham unable to bowl, Wharton's declaration enabled Nottinghamshire to storm to a seven-wicket victory on what Jack stresses was a featherbed pitch. Eighty-six against Leicestershire, fifties against Warwickshire and Essex and a pair of half-centuries in Lancashire's second match against the tourists at Blackpool concluded a more satisfactory summer for Jack, his first-class average rising to a respectable 31.92 for his 862 runs.

The next season, Bob Barber's first in charge after the retirement of Washbrook, was another in Jack's switchback fortunes, with long periods in and out of the side as Booth, Bolton and Collins were all given their chances. A century against the South Africans, followed in the next match by another undefeated hundred against Somerset at Old Trafford, were the highlights of a summer that also had its lean spells. Runs still came in the second team and Jack was recalled for the last five first-team matches to witness a season that had promised a glorious climax conclude with Lancashire's aspirations in tatters. Leading the table comfortably in early August, with the extra satisfaction of having beaten Yorkshire twice, the county could muster only eight points from their last six matches, ceding the title to their White Rose rivals by the comfortable margin of 32 points.

The Lancashire team which finished second in the Championship in 1960.
Standing (l to r): J.D.Bond, K.Higgs, G.Pullar, R.Collins, P.T.Marner, B.J.Booth,
K.Goodwin (wk).
Seated: K.J.Grieves, A.Wharton, R.W.Barber (capt), J.B.Statham,
T.Greenhough.
G.Clayton, the regular wicket-keeper, is missing.

The following year Lancashire would drop to thirteenth in the table, but for Jack it was a fine season, the first in which he held a regular place in the county side all summer. His self-belief received a boost in the fourth match, against the Australians at Old Trafford, when an innings of 68 earned him his county cap. Like Roy Collins, who had also been on the staff for several seasons and was capped at the same time, Jack had been wondering if he could continue for much longer as a fringe player. 'It had reached the situation where they either had to give us our county caps or sack us. Getting your county cap, it suddenly made you think that other people believed in you, the people that were actually controlling your lives. That did spur the pair of us on.' By the end of the summer he had hit 1,701 runs in all matches with three centuries.

In mid-August, against Sussex at Old Trafford, Jack reached three figures in 93 minutes. With a prize of £250 on offer from the *Evening Standard* for the fastest first-day century, his 106 included four sixes and outstripped his friend Collins, whose hundred against Gloucestershire only a week earlier had taken an hour and three quarters. Collins had insured himself against being overtaken for a modest premium of some £12 and was able to collect his money from the insurers, while Jack wondered if he should risk it as the season had only a couple of weeks to run. In the end caution won the day, but the insurers, having burnt their fingers once, asked him to pay £75. So his net profit was only £175, still enough to justify a celebration party after the last game, against Kent at Blackpool. 'Kent are party animals,' says Jack, 'one or two mad people, so we had a heck of a good party at the Savoy Hotel where both teams were staying.'

Jack's other hundreds came against Cambridge University and late in the season at Bath, when he hit 152 after Lancashire had conceded a first-innings lead of 202 to Somerset. Saving the match was Jack's sole priority when he came in, but his later runs were harvested with greater ease once it became clear that there would be no declaration and wicket-keeper Harold Stephenson took his pads off to bowl.

Lancashire's problems multiplied in 1962, when Barber was replaced as captain by Joe Blackledge, a captain with no first-class experience, under whom the county plunged to sixteenth place in the Championship. But for Jack it was his most prolific summer. It started in April with a place in MCC's side to take on Yorkshire, the champion county, at Lord's. Though he made few runs on this occasion, Jack found in his new county captain a man who believed in him. Given a regular spot at number three, he was soon repaying his skipper's faith. In the second match, at Derby, he played his part in a brave run-chase that was just thwarted when 14 were needed with Les Jackson to bowl the final over. Sixty-nine against Kent helped to secure first-innings points, then at Southampton his skipper's declaration came with Jack still at the wicket on 96. 'I hadn't had any signal saying what was happening. He just clapped his hands and I walked in. He declared with quarter of an hour to go to lunch and I was on 96. We came off and we bowled for five minutes, two overs.'

Blackledge's challenge set Hampshire, the reigning champions, to make 318 at 79 an hour. In the words of *The Times*, the declaration was 'a delicate piece of timing.' A splendid match ended in a three-wicket win for the home team off the fourth ball of the final over. At the death, Joe Blackledge's bowlers failed him. There was a muddle over a crucial run out, and the luck the new captain so badly needed ran against him, as it would all summer.

Soon Jack was scoring runs as never before. In four matches he had three centuries: 109 against the Pakistanis; 118 off the Essex bowlers; then 144 in the Roses Match at Leeds. There was a career-best 157 against Hampshire and another Roses hundred later in the season as he became the second batsman in the country to pass 2,000 runs, reaching the landmark one hour after Roy Marshall. As Jack points out, such records can come more readily in a weak side: 'We nearly always fielded once and batted twice – we were that sort of a side. I must have had 60 innings.' Very true – he had 67 in all first-class matches. His name was mentioned as a possible for the tour of Australia, though he was not among the 29 players to whom availability enquiries were sent.

At the peak of his career as a batsman that summer, Jack awaited the 1963 season with rare confidence. But it was not long before his high hopes were to be dashed. In only the second match, against the West Indian tourists at Old Trafford, he suffered an injury that would blight the rest of his career. He had made 21 in the first innings and, when Lancashire were asked to follow on, he was very soon back at the crease. Both openers had been dismissed for ducks and Jack was engaged with his new captain, Ken Grieves, in a rearguard action to save the match. On 26 he was facing Wes Hall, perhaps the most feared fast bowler of his day, when a short-pitched ball reared up at him. 'You're always taught to watch the ball even when you duck. I put my hand up and it hit my wrist.' Jack's arm went numb and he was in obvious pain, but he chuckles at the memory of umpire Charlie Elliott's advice when he had to admit that he couldn't hold the bat and would have to go off. 'He said, "You may as well, Jack. After all, it's only a friendly match!"'

A bad break was later diagnosed. His wrist in plaster, Jack played no cricket for nine weeks. There was one game with the second eleven in mid-July, bringing 44 against Derbyshire, before he was

*Jack returning to the pavilion at Old Trafford, after his second century of the
1962 season against the champion county, Yorkshire.
This photograph was taken by Jim Hardy, his old primary school teacher.*

*Jack hits out, in darkening conditions, against the Pakistanis at Old Trafford in
July 1962. The wicket-keeper is Ijaz Butt.*

restored to the first team – too early, he now admits. 'I wasn't strong enough or fit enough. It took me about eighteen months before I could pick up a shovel full of coal and throw it on the fire.' There were a couple of thirties, but a string of low scores saw Jack end the season a second-team player once more. His side's best batsman just twelve months earlier, he was now looking at a career under threat.

While Jack's star had risen to new heights in 1962, the fortunes of Lancashire had plumbed hitherto unthinkable depths. A team that had achieved its best post-war results under Nigel Howard had slid back under Cyril Washbrook, threatened to take the title as soon as Bob Barber replaced him, but had fallen back to what was then its lowest-ever point in the second season of Barber's captaincy. Thirteenth spot that year belied a fair record of nine victories against only seven defeats, but the following summer the luckless Joe Blackledge presided over a side whose points tally dropped from 142 to just 60, only a Leicestershire side in parallel disarray depriving Lancashire of the wooden spoon. It would be a long haul back towards respectability, the next five seasons seeing a rise of just one place each year as first Ken Grieves and then Brian Statham assumed the captaincy.

Looking back, Jack finds it hard to credit how well the side had done in the early months of Barber's captaincy. So much was against a man whom Jack grew to respect and like. 'Bob was very unlucky,' he says. 'When he first captained Lancashire he'd never really lived in the outside world.' Jack also recalls Barber playing for Cambridge against the county: 'He batted a heck of a long time and I can remember Cyril saying, "This lad will never captain Lancashire." Cyril didn't seem to like him at all – I don't know what it was.'

However, the cult of the amateur captain was still alive, some counties going to ludicrous extremes to find a young man with social credentials that could be passed off as leadership qualities. By 1960 Barber was a player of proven worth, so his appointment became a formality. Yet he took over without endorsement from his predecessor, and he had already suffered, as so many amateurs did, from the resentment of professionals who had to make way or see a friend drop out when he was picked to play. Jack was one who suffered this fate: 'As soon as Bob came back, I would drop out of the side. It happened with David Green as well.' Losing money in consequence, Jack could understand his team-mates' attitude.

In truth, the professionals in the Lancashire dressing room wanted a captain from within their own circle. To compound his problems, Barber bowed to a committee edict that he should stay in a different hotel from his team, counsel that was opposed by no less a man than Major Rupert Howard, the former secretary and father of Nigel, whose view was that 'it was out of touch with modern practice in first-class cricket.' Jack strongly agrees: 'Not staying with the team was a big mistake. I think you learn far more about people – and you need to learn about them – off the field.'

As success eluded the team in the final weeks of this first season, the captain had already become aware of off-the-field problems, where there was a disunited committee and a weak chairman. 'There were at least two camps in the club,' he says, 'and I was not aware that I ever had a camp!' A young, slightly introverted captain, with problems in his dressing room, desperately needed support, yet Bob was left exposed by his committee. He was most aware of this when, attempting to defend remarks made by Ken Grieves, he spoke naively to a journalist after Kent had failed to respond to his challenge in a match at Old Trafford. A supposed spat between Colin Cowdrey and a player who had made a disappointing Test debut under his captaincy earlier that summer made good headlines for the popular press!

At the end the season the committee decided to offer vice-captain Alan Wharton the chance to lead the second team. Effectively this meant they were sacking him as a first-team player. And it happened without the captain being consulted. Moreover, without Wharton, who chose to extend his first-class career by moving to Leicestershire, Barber was deprived of the man who had been in charge of the players off the field. It also meant that only Grieves now remained of the batsmen from the early 1950s. With Statham, Higgs and Greenhough, Barber had a potentially strong attack in 1961, but Greenhough was destined to miss most of the season with a damaged finger, while the loss of Wharton meant that there was a more uncertain look to the batting, though it would be eased by Jack's timely advance.

One poor season spelled the end of Bob Barber's captaincy. The news that he was to be replaced after just two seasons was conveyed to the deposed skipper through a cable sent to Tom

Pearce, manager of the MCC team with which he was touring India and Pakistan. There was no letter of thanks or explanation.

Bob now looks back sadly on a period in his career when cricket gave him little pleasure. His sorrow is the greater for his belief that he inherited a talented team that could have won Championships for Lancashire. He speaks, for instance, of Pullar as 'the most beautiful left-handed off-side – yes, off-side – player I had seen,' of Marner as having 'more to offer, a width of ability, a greater range of shots, than Ted Dexter at an early stage' and of Greenhough as 'richly talented and a wonderful team man'. Though he had already felt himself less welcome in the dressing room once he had become the captain in waiting, and despite regrets at the enforced distancing from his team, he still says: 'To the many immensely talented cricketers who played under me in the 60s, I have nothing but fond memories and abiding affection.'

Bob Barber acknowledges benefiting from an initial impetus when he first took charge of a side glad to see the back of Washbrook, a man with the county's best interests at heart, but too strict a disciplinarian for many of his players. Bob remains proud of his first few months in charge, but he believes that his side was thwarted by Old Trafford pitches that were too good to produce results and he points to the weather, as so often, frustrating Lancashire in August. He also admits to a divided dressing room in which 'the heavy brigade', as a group of players styled themselves, could lead younger team-mates astray, though one man on whom he could count was Jack: 'Jackie always gave me the impression that he was a decent, well-balanced man. He was friendly to all. He didn't get involved with the "heavy brigade" off the field. Yet he enjoyed a beer, got on pleasantly with everybody and was 100% a team man. A decent bat, he would attack or defend as circumstances dictated, a splendid field; a good man. What else do you want?'

Bob expands on what he strove for at Old Trafford: 'I wanted a team of 100% committed professionals whose clear objective was to develop their own and the team's abilities. It called for some control of the "good time" element without losing the fun of playing. It required not just a captain who wished for it, but for all the club to be kicking in the same direction.'

The committee at this time included some good men, Bob felt, 'but also too many wanting to boost their businesses or their egos so they could say, "I am a member of the Lancashire Committee."' Committee workings were seen to worst effect when it came to team selection. He formed the impression that members of all committees, and perhaps vice-presidents as well, had their penny's worth at the Selection Committee deliberations. They met at 3pm, amply wined and dined and, when they were ready to pronounce, the captain was summoned. 'I was astonished by my first experience,' Bob says. 'Vino tended to make even those of limited cricket background rather vociferous! Thirty to forty around a table!'

For the second year of his captaincy, at Bob's instigation, a different structure was introduced, with a selection committee of three: a chairman, Frank Sibbles, coach Stan Worthington and the captain. However, the new arrangement did not prevent the captain receiving a message that, at a time when Statham was absent on Test duty, he was to send Ken Higgs home for a rest. Though he had shown poorer form than in 1960, Higgs' own view of the matter was that it was because he needed more bowling!

After such experiences, Bob admits that 'some of my enthusiasm and my interest in the captaincy died.' A couple of years later, after he had made his move to Warwickshire, Ken Grieves, then the Lancashire skipper, invited Bob for 'a beer and a bite' with Brian Statham and himself. 'That evening they both said to me – and there was no reason for Brian to do so – that they were deeply sorry for all that had happened. "We did not realise until now what you had to put up with." A treasured memory!'

Having decided to relieve Bob Barber of the captaincy, in what was to be the last year of the amateur in English cricket, the committee turned to a 34-year-old club cricketer as captain. They hoped that Joe Blackledge might achieve for Lancashire what Ronnie Burnet had managed when he had taken control of a divided Yorkshire team and won the Championship in his second season. Blackledge was not quite the lame duck he has sometimes been painted. In 33 games for the second team in the early 1950s he had averaged 35 with two centuries. But his last match had been in 1953 and he had no experience of the first-class game.

'If they'd wanted him to captain the side, it should have been five or six years earlier,' says Jack, looking back on a dismal chapter in the history of a great club. 'Bob Barber had had no support from the senior professionals, none at all. They didn't want him – they wanted one of their own. Of course it made it even worse when they appointed Joe.' Ken Grieves, who had been eyeing the captaincy for himself, departed. Barber, preferring to avoid a charge of sour grapes, stayed on.

Lancashire's captains.
Bob Barber, in 1960 and 1961, and Joe Blackledge in 1962.

Blackledge did his best. 'He had a hard time,' says Jack, 'and he was a lovely fellow. You could sense that he felt everything was against him, various instructions from the committee and so forth, but he never let it get him down.' With only two championship matches won while 16 were lost, poor Joe Blackledge lasted just one season before Ken Grieves was persuaded out of his brief retirement to take on the job he had yearned for some time.

Jack always regarded the new captain as a fine batsman and a man who enjoyed the game. He was a knowledgeable cricketer, Jack felt, and one who came in determined to prove the committee wrong in not appointing him earlier. But Grieves would soon learn that the object of his ambition was a poisoned chalice. He continued to preside over an unhappy dressing room, and his first season brought little success on the field with only Marner and the captain himself passing a thousand runs. Of the principal run-getters from the previous summer, Barber had departed to Warwickshire, where his love for the game was restored, Pullar had returned injured from Australia, played in fewer than half the matches and showed little form, while Jack, the reliable number three, had broken his wrist at the start of the campaign.

Worse was to come for Lancashire and for Grieves, but for Jack, as his frustrating season drew to a close, the priority was to get the strength back into his wrist. So, when a proposition came his way that would allow him to escape the gloom of an English winter and perhaps help the mending process, he leapt at the chance.

Chapter Five

'A Methodist coaching the Catholics'

Brian Booth, three years younger than Jack, had been on the ground staff when he arrived and first won a regular place in the county side in 1961. Joining Lancashire principally as a leg-spinner, he had gradually developed his batting and had become a regular opener. Booth was a man with whom Jack shared a room for away matches. On Sundays the pair would both go off to church – but in different directions, Jack seeking out his fellow Methodists, while his friend made for a Roman Catholic church.

Booth had spent a number of winters coaching at the Christian Brothers College at Kimberley in South Africa but, when he found himself unable to return at the end of the 1963 season, he offered Jack the chance to deputise. 'A Methodist coaching the Catholics!' The thought that a follower of Wesley should take the job appealed to Jack's sense of humour. He lost little time in accepting.

His South African adventure was a far cry from some of Jack's earlier winter jobs. Finding off-season work has always been a problem for cricketers. For those on Lancashire's books in Jack's time, it could be doubly difficult as the county paid its players a nominal sum, fifty pounds for the whole winter, which allowed the club to retain their insurance cards and pay the weekly stamp. Perhaps there was generous intent behind the gesture, but it meant that the cricketers were precluded from signing on for unemployment benefit. They *had* to find work.

In his first winter as a player with Lancashire, Jack had discovered to his surprise that he could not re-join his previous employers. 'I'd thought I'm a cricketer now, they'll surely want me. You get a bit big-headed, don't you?' With two years in the Pay Corps he could point to wide clerical experience. 'I thought I'll be able to get any job, but NALGO said "Oh, no. He's got a job. Cricket's his job. We're taking on somebody that's out of work."'

There had been a winter looking after hire purchase agreements for a television dealer, but working on Saturdays was alien to Jack:

'I was usually going to watch football. Suddenly I couldn't go.' He worked in the fish-and-chip shop and later in the café that replaced it, serving meals to the workers in the local cotton mill. Another winter job entailed a 5.30 start, marshalling all the lorries that queued to load up with Christmas goods from the GUS warehouse in Farnworth. 'I was the Receiving Officer – sounds a bit dodgy, doesn't it?'

Bidding farewell to Florence, who was to join him for Christmas, Jack sailed out to South Africa on the ageing *R.M.S. Pretoria Castle* – it had a permanent list to one side, he remembers. On what was his first venture overseas, he was accompanied by a dozen English professionals who had taken winter coaching jobs. He shared a cabin with Paul Gibb, a one-time Cambridge Blue who had played for Yorkshire and Essex and whom he now knew as a first-class umpire. 'I had the top bunk and he had the bottom.' In their cramped cabin there was only one drawer each and Jack remembers that Gibb's was full of pills and tablets. 'What he was taking them all for, I don't know, because he was as thin as a rake.' Gibb was not the most sociable of companions, preferring to lie in the sun rather than take part in deck games and other amusements. 'He hardly said a word the whole trip. I can remember him always being first into the restaurant and always being last out – because he always finished up not with a dish of ice cream but a canister, a catering canister.'

Once he had settled in at the Christian Brothers College, Jack's mornings were devoted to net sessions for boys of different ages throughout the school who came during their games period; in the afternoon he would be with the first team. On Saturdays Jack played with his boys as they competed in a men's league. There were six teams in the division, four men's clubs and two schools, but while the schools were inviolate, one of the clubs would be relegated at the end of the season. With points scored against the schools always important to their opponents, Jack was struck by how competitive the matches were. 'I think this is one of the reasons why South Africans mature a lot quicker than our boys. They would be only 14 or 15 and they were playing in the men's league. The game was played very hard and you found out very quickly who was going to be good enough. And the way that these lads fielded – they chased everything to the boundary.'

Jack also believes that, although all the matches were played on grass, the boys benefited from practising on matting. 'The nets were rolled sand and matting. It made them play – that's why these lads were better movers, quicker movers than our lads because batting on the mat, it does make you think, like you had to on the uncovered wickets I was brought up on. They were less predictable and you had to learn to make adjustments. And that quickness of eye and feet is what's missing today.'

Jack proved a popular coach and he was asked back for the following two winters, taking the family with him on both occasions. Jack and Florence now had two children – Stephanie, born in 1956, and Wesley, four years younger. While Wesley's name reflects the family's Methodist roots, Stephanie owes hers to Jack's cricketing idol from his teenage days. In 1948 he had seen Lindsay Hassett play at Old Trafford, and the sight of another conspicuously small man had been an inspiration to him. Had their first child been a boy, he would have been christened Lindsay Stuart, but when a girl arrived a compromise was reached by retaining the chosen initials and naming her Lynn Stephanie. 'We fancied Stephanie more than Lynn, so that's what we called her right from the word go.'

Brothers Macinerny (left) and McDonald greet Jack and Florence at Kimberley station in 1964, when Stephanie and Wesley accompanied them on their return to the Christian Brothers College.

In Kimberley Wesley was able to attend the College's junior school, but Stephanie's education was more of a concern as she was approaching the age for senior school. However, she thrived at the local convent and Jack believes that travel and the experience of life in another country more than compensated for what his children may have lost in formal education.

For his first trip Jack had been in a bed-and-breakfast hotel but, when he returned with the family, they boarded with an elderly landlady who had just one drawback: 'She didn't feed us very well. Sometimes we'd only get corn on the cob with some bread and butter and that would be it.' At times they would supplement their meal at a café down the road, but there were also invitations to join the brothers at the college.

For their third and final trip, when the family had their own bungalow adjacent to the college cricket field, Jack became most conscious of the abnormal society in which he was living. The notion that black people should be segregated on buses and shut away in their own townships at night was abhorrent to his Methodist instincts. In their small way he and Florence did what they could to befriend their house boy and maids and ensure that they had enough food to take home, but beyond that they felt in no position to do very much about it.

Returning to Britain on RMS Edinburgh Castle, with (l to r) Don Shepherd, Don Bates, Dennis A'Court and their wives.

One black man of whom Jack grew fond was William, the college employee who helped prepare the pitches. One weekend Jack gave his assistant a few rand – it was worth about two pounds, he reckons – and William never turned up for work for the next two days. 'He'll have been boozed up,' Jack was told. A lesson was learned: 'In the future, if I gave him a tip, I made sure it wasn't the day before a match!'

'Going to church didn't resolve anything,' Jack adds sadly of the apartheid that surrounded him. 'We were just uncomfortable, but we weren't living in fear.' Despite the emotional discomfort life in the South African sunshine had many compensations, sufficient to kindle thoughts of emigrating; but both Jack and Florence had widowed mothers back in England and they were loath to be so far away from them.

For the 1964 season changes were in the air at Old Trafford. Brian Booth had moved on to Leicestershire and there were new faces competing for places in the batting line-up. David Green, who had first appeared while at Oxford, was now a full-time cricketer and another Oxford Blue, Duncan Worsley, came into the side after the Varsity match. Bob Bennett, a former amateur who had enjoyed a long run the previous year, now played fewer matches, as did Jack Dyson and the young Harry Pilling, but a regular place for most of the summer was found for Bob Entwistle from Burnley.

This was also the first year in which Lancashire appointed a manager for the first team; Cyril Washbrook, now a committee member, took on the mantle, usually with George Duckworth at his side. Though Washbrook accompanied the side to most of their away matches, Jack has no recollection of the former skipper giving any rousing speeches or holding team meetings. 'He was acting more as an observer.'

Jack was still hampered by the injury to his wrist and it was a struggle to reproduce the form he had shown before his accident. He started the summer in the first team and scored a fast century in a first-day run feast against Hampshire, but after only nine championship matches he was back in the second team. He recalls how he lost his place after two failures in the match at Derby. 'I got out twice playing the late cut, one of my run-scoring shots in my good years.'

Though Jack describes his dab as 'a shot that Washbrook lived on', he feels that it led to his exclusion from the team. No-one said so directly – it was not the way things were done in those days – but Jack was taken into the captain's room after the match, where he learned that he was to be dropped, and Washbrook expressed the view that, with a lot of young players about, he was unlikely to get back. Captaincy of the second team on a regular basis was offered.

'But I turned that down,' Jack says, 'because I still believed that I had something to offer as a first-class player. I didn't want to be appointed and forgotten about. A number of committee people had written me off.' With an average of almost 28, his first-eleven record compared favourably with most of the other fringe players, but it was still second-eleven cricket for the rest of the season and, in his unofficial position as captain, it was Jack who could take most of the credit for leading the side to a fine double as Lancashire won both the Second Eleven and Minor Counties Championships.

These successes contrasted with the fortunes of the senior side, for whom climbing one place up the table was scant compensation for a season that ended in unparalleled disarray. To disappointments on the field were now added revelations of indiscipline that led to the sacking of Marner and Clayton, while Dyson was released because he was thought to be 'not now up to the playing standard required.' Out, too, went the captain Grieves.

It was all clumsily handled, with the four sackings reaching the ears of the public before the players had been told. Jim Cumbes, now Chief Executive at Old Trafford, was a 20-year-old on twelfth-man duty when the news broke. 'They didn't find out till they read the newspaper in the dressing room. I was the twelfth man for that match and you can imagine the language that was flying round. It had been leaked by one of the committee. I thought, "What shall I do – go out or carry on pouring the drinks?" I can see them now sitting on the bench reading the paper – in the middle of a match.'

Though the cricket committee had earlier required that 'Bond be asked to submit to a medical examination,' Jack's position at Old Trafford was the stronger for the loss of so many senior players. 'I was lucky that Lancashire had a poor season and it all blew up with the wholesale sackings.' Moreover, a later committee minute reveals that he was seen as 'a very good influence on the younger players,' while discussions about coaching positions also saw his name mentioned.

There was more clumsiness in trying to find a successor to Grieves with a box numbered advertisement in *The Times*, which was easily identified as relating to Lancashire. There were overtures to A.C.Smith at Warwickshire and suggestions that Cheshire's Freddie Millett might be persuaded to step in for a year. Nothing materialised and, with some misgivings, the committee turned to Brian Statham, the player whose Test match deeds set him apart from the rest of the staff, and a man who had kept his distance from the worst of the rows and recriminations, while plying his trade of bowling fast, straight and successfully.

Even before the sackings it was widely known that morale was as low as it had been for many years in the first-team dressing room, where the senior players were reluctant to welcome newcomers into their circle. 'Senior professionals protecting senior professionals,' says Jack, 'thinking that a young professional was threatening one of their mates' positions – that did go on.' Some of the young hopefuls, in turn, found the atmosphere distasteful and had little wish to be picked, preferring life in the second team as Peter Lever, who had joined the county in 1960, recalls: 'The teams went up on a little notice board where the junior pros were housed. "Oh, so and so is in the first team. Bad luck, son!"'

Jack well remembers senior players trying to rid themselves of any threat that Bob Bennett might pose. Against Cambridge University, a challenging Fenner's pitch had reduced Lancashire to 69 for seven in their first innings. They recovered to 183 all out, after which they bowled the students out for 181. The county then had to bat a second time on a pitch that was still asking questions of the batsmen. 'One or two people were thinking the best way of getting rid of Bob was to send him in first, he gets out and that's that. So Bob went in first and got a hundred – absolutely brilliant. They weren't thinking of him succeeding – they were only thinking of him failing and he didn't!'

There was a decisive twist to the shenanigans when disaffected members called for an Extraordinary General Meeting. By an overwhelming majority they registered that they were 'dissatisfied with the conduct of the cricketing affairs of the club.' Elections brought fresh blood to the committee and before long the instigator of the rebellion, Manchester businessman Cedric Rhoades, was installed as chairman. A new era had begun, but there was much still to be put right.

Meanwhile, knowing that the committee felt unsure about him, Jack had left for South Africa with a firm offer of a coaching job at a school in Norfolk to chew over. He had taken the opportunity to write a personal note to the Secretary, Geoffrey Howard, himself in his last months before moving to The Oval, warning of his impending resignation and taking the opportunity to express his feelings about what was wrong with Lancashire, notably the salary structure and length of contract. 'The basic should have been increased and a lower match fee paid. They were working to a structure that made the rest of the players the poor relations to those in the first team, and it had an effect on team spirit.'

'I'd be most upset if you chose to leave,' the widely respected Geoffrey Howard replied. There was a positive response to Jack's observations, with players being given more security through longer contracts. Deciding to soldier on, Jack spent most of the next two years as he had for so much of his time – on the fringe of the first team, often watching on while others, mostly players he had guided in his successful second team, were given their chance. In 1965 he played 15 first-team matches, while Mike Beddow, Harry Pilling and John Sullivan each played 21, Gerry Knox 19, and debutants David Lloyd and Ken Snellgrove 13 and 14 respectively. Most of these players struggled and, in another low-scoring season, each Lancashire wicket in the Championship averaged no more than 18.72, making Jack's modest 19.82 good enough to give him fifth spot in the championship list. Holding a place in the team until mid-June but then playing only twice more, his best scores were an undefeated 112 in a losing cause at Leicester and 95 in the defeat of Sussex at Liverpool.

When not on first-team duty Jack captained the Second Eleven, but he and his charges were less successful than in 1964, and in 1966 the second team captaincy was handed to Bob Bennett, under whom Jack played a handful of matches. A century against Yorkshire Second Eleven showed that he was in good form and by early June he was back in the first team, where he held his place for the rest of the season.

Chapter Six

'We need someone to read nine verses'

Jack's championship average in 1966 was a modest 23.77. In a season where runs were unusually hard to come by across the country, the Lancashire batting was among the weakest, and Jack's figures were bettered only by Worsley, who had won his cap after dropping down the order, and Pullar, whose meagre 30.82 brought him the top spot. Meanwhile Green endured a poor summer, Knox held a regular place without advancing, and Pilling did not maintain his promise, while other younger players given chances – David Lloyd, Barry Wood and John Sullivan – were still finding their feet in the first-class game.

Despite a rise of one place in the table to twelfth, the malaise at Old Trafford went deeper than the frailty of the batting line-up. There was improving support for Statham and Higgs from pace bowlers Ken Shuttleworth and Peter Lever, but a lean year for Tommy Greenhough ended with another talented cricketer added to the long list of those whose time with Lancashire came to an untimely and disenchanted end. 'Leaving Lancashire virtually destroyed him. Tommy lived for cricket and his leg-spin bowling,' says Jack, of a player he held in high regard as a cricketer and a man. With Ken Howard also deciding to take leave of the first-class game, there were no spin bowlers left at Old Trafford.

Morale remained low. Speaking perhaps primarily of the days before the 1964 revolution, Greenhough was recorded as saying: 'There was too much interference on team selection from committee men. Too often we went onto the field knowing it wasn't our strongest team.' Batsmen, in particular, were known to play for themselves, allowing their end-of-season average to take precedence over the needs of the team. Jack certainly formed this view of some of his team-mates: 'They were playing for themselves – without a doubt. It was the self-protection racket. On occasions you'd be suspicious with somebody running somebody else out in your own side. It's a sad thing to say, but professional jealousy is an awful thing, and that did go on for quite a long time.'

In Jack's view, the captain should have argued the case for retaining Greenhough, but this was an aspect of captaincy that Brian Statham found distasteful, and he hated confrontation. 'He was such a nice, mild-mannered man. I can understand that he didn't want the hassle of committee meetings and that side of it. He would find it difficult if he had twelve people to pick eleven out of that twelve. He would find it very, very hard to say to someone, "Look, sorry but … ." The job of leaving people out, that would upset him.'

The ambivalent skipper, perhaps the only man who could have taken the job on, Jack feels, had started with a vice-captain, David Green, who was widely seen as a logical successor. The cricket committee had been unanimous in putting forward the name of the former Oxford Blue in 1965, and that summer he passed 2,000 runs in first-class matches. However, he was never the type to bow uncritically to authority and aspects of his behaviour had been a topic for discussion in committee. By 1966 he was 'not a suitable candidate for the captaincy'. Matters did not improve and the committee resolved that he would not continue as vice-captain.

Initially they were minded to give the vice-captaincy to Pullar, but he was no longer the inspirational figure he had once been. Since his return from Australia in 1963 his batting had suffered along with his health. In 1965 doubts about his long-term future were expressed when it had been resolved that he should be told before the start of the next season that 'he should really get down to it and get himself fully fit and make himself a really invaluable member of the side.' Eventually no vice-captain was appointed for 1967, but it was agreed that Pullar should 'take over at any time the captain had to leave the field of play during the course of a match.'

Meanwhile steps were taken to recruit players from outside the county. This was not the traditional Red Rose approach. Indeed, back in 1956 when 'the captain had drawn attention to the ability of a young cricketer at present playing for the Cambridge University eleven,' it was resolved that 'the Club's policy with regard to the playing of Lancashire-born cricketers should be followed and no approach should be made to E.R.Dexter.'

To fill the spin-bowling gap a player older than the departing Greenhough was recruited. Ramsbottom-born John Savage, an off-spinner, had played second-eleven cricket for Lancashire in the

1950s but, seeing little chance of breaking into the first team, he had moved to Leicestershire, where he had played for 14 seasons. The batting was also strengthened by the winter signing of 29-year-old Graham Atkinson. Offered no more than a one-year contract by Somerset, whose batting he had opened for the past decade, the Yorkshire-born Atkinson had opted to try his luck elsewhere.

At a pre-season committee meeting Cedric Rhoades had favoured giving the second-eleven captaincy to Jack, had it not been that 'Bond would automatically think he was being ruled out for First XI selection if he was offered the appointment.' In fact, the arrival of Atkinson meant that there was no first team place for Jack in a side whose top six to start the season read: Atkinson, Green, Pilling, Worsley, Pullar, Sullivan.

In 'the wettest May since 1773', these six saw the county through the first three championship games – two rain-spoilt draws and a heavy loss to Middlesex. Jack's name was then included in the squad for the first of three successive matches at Old Trafford that were rained off without a ball bowled, with *Wisden* recording that, for the last two, the players did not even come to the ground. Only a switch to Southport, not permitted for championship matches, saved the fixture with the Indian tourists.

With Atkinson and Green missing from the side for Lancashire's next match at Trent Bridge, Pullar and Wood opened the batting, and Jack regained his place at number five. An undefeated 36 to secure a draw kept him in the team for the next match, against Derbyshire at Old Trafford. With Pullar and Statham absent as well as Green, Jack led the side for the first time. Another draw was described by *Wisden* as 'a slow-motion match in which the tactics of the rival captains, Bond and Morgan, caused much discussion and criticism. The players lacked a sense of aggression on a pitch and outfield still drying out from weeks of heavy rain.'

Jack understands the criticism, but this was a match in which he felt a new scoring system awarded too many points for a first-innings lead rather than providing incentive to push for outright victory. Despite having a strong pace attack – Harold Rhodes and Brian Jackson were two of the country's leading bowlers that summer – Derbyshire quickly went on the defensive, captain Derek Morgan's field placings bent only on saving runs. 'It was sheer bloody-mindedness,' Jack still feels. But late in the final afternoon, Jack got his reward when Derbyshire's last wicket fell with the visitors still four short of Lancashire's 301 for seven. 'It was a shame for the spectators,' he reflects. 'The people who turned up that Sunday must have been bored to death.'

An undefeated 78 in the second innings of the return match with Derbyshire at Buxton, followed by 97 against Sussex at Old Trafford, helped cement Jack's place in the senior side, and he was captain again when Lancashire won a far from one-sided game against Oxford University, making a much needed 69 not out. Significantly, Jack was appointed captain for this match, despite the presence of both Pullar and Green.

He remained as captain against Surrey when, batting on for one over after lunch on the final day, he 'did not make his challenge attractive enough and Surrey slowly batted out time.' At Folkestone he presided over a heavy Lancashire defeat, after which Statham returned to take charge once more. For Jack the runs had now started to dry up. Though there was a brave undefeated 33 out of 129 against Glamorgan, he registered a pair against Somerset as Lancashire narrowly escaped heavy defeat.

Jack was then omitted from the side for the visit of Middlesex, but he took over as skipper in a friendly match against Scotland, when he declared twice without going to the crease himself at a time when he was badly in need of some batting practice. Left out of the side against Northamptonshire, he returned against Hampshire to make a third consecutive duck on a Blackpool pitch 'of variable pace and bounce' on which the visitors later collapsed for just 39. Not asked to play in the county's next matches, he was once again wondering whether his years as a Lancashire player might have been coming to an end.

Jack has been quick to acknowledge the moments in his career when Providence has been on his side, not least the well-concealed date of birth when he had first presented himself at the Secretary's office. Now he was to enjoy another lucky break. The Lancashire team was scheduled to set off for a three-match tour taking in games against Gloucestershire, Worcestershire and Essex. The Gloucestershire match was to be played at Cheltenham College as part of the annual Festival.

To mark the occasion the College had arranged a sportsmen's service for the Sunday, at which it was hoped a Lancashire player would read a lesson of nine verses in the chapel. The prospect had no appeal to Statham and no other player was keen to volunteer. 'So it was suggested that I went as twelfth man – to read these nine verses,' Jack now recalls. 'I wouldn't have gone as twelfth man without reading the nine verses – somebody else would have gone and played if anyone had been injured.'

Though his Methodist upbringing will have prepared Jack for his time at the lectern, the prospect of reading in the college chapel still caused him some anxiety: 'John Savage and myself were sat up in bed till four o'clock in the morning while I'm rehearsing the nine verses. I'll never forget it. We'd been up with Geoff Edrich, who was coach and groundsman at Cheltenham. Geoff had taken us to The Highwayman and was telling us all these stories.'

Meanwhile the Gloucestershire match proved a game of tilting fortunes that ended with Lancashire, twice rescued with the bat by Shuttleworth, striving in the extra half-hour for the last Gloucestershire wicket. But for Jack, with the bible reading ordeal behind him, there is one dominating memory: the time he had to spend on the field. Pullar had made 64 in Lancashire's total of 284, but when his turn came to field the former Test batsman had been less enthusiastic. 'I'm on and off that field all day,' Jack recalls, 'and by the time we got into the dressing room, he's out through the gate on his way to Worcester. And when we got to Worcester the same thing happened again. I'm up and down them steps all the time when we're fielding and Geoff is coming on and off. And when we were getting ready to go down to Chelmsford, there's Geoff Pullar packing his bags in his little MG and Brian Statham said, "Where do you think you're going?" He said, "I'm going to Chelmsford. I've got someone to see down there. I've arranged to go to dinner. So I'm off now." Brian said, "No, you're not – you can get in your car and go back home!" So he sent Geoff back home.'

Pullar had top-scored with 44 in Lancashire's first innings, but his inability or unwillingness to do his stint in the field had tested his captain's patience beyond what even the mild-mannered, unconfrontational Statham could take. It was one of the boldest moves of his captaincy. 'So they had to pick me,' says Jack. 'There wasn't time to get anybody else down. So that's how my luck ran.'

At Chelmsford there was 'a brisk display' bringing Jack 64 useful runs as Lancashire built on the platform of a Graham Atkinson century. His top-scoring 37 then saved the second innings from disintegration to set up a 24-run victory achieved with seven minutes to spare. As the match reached its climax, with Robin Hobbs and David Acfield at the crease and Statham and Shuttleworth striving for the last wicket, Jack played a crucial part: 'It looked as though Essex were going to get away with a draw. Brian was always reluctant to bowl a bouncer. He was afraid of hurting people as much as anything. So when we got it the right way round and Ken was bowling at Acfield, I said "Come on, Shutt, you've got to let him have one." And he bowled him one and Acfield looked at Ken as if to say, "This is not on, bowling it at tailenders" – the old university attitude. Well Ken bowled him another one and there was arms and gloves and everything. It popped up for an easy catch and we all walked off the field with the game won.'

For their fifth championship win of the summer Lancashire could thank the little battler from Bolton. Fourth in the championship averages behind Pilling, Pullar and Atkinson with 27.26, he had earned his retention. Though few could have guessed it, his best years lay ahead.

Chapter Seven
'You'll have to have all your teeth out'

The 1968 season was to be the last of Brian Statham's distinguished career with Lancashire. He had led the county for three seasons, taking his team one place up the championship table each year, and had now accepted a sales position with Guinness. His new job was to start at the end of the summer, and he preferred to bow out of cricket without the burden of captaincy.

In their search for the man to replace Statham, Lancashire's first reaction, as it had been in 1964, was to look outside for candidates. Coincidentally this was the year in which regulations were to be eased to permit the counties to recruit an overseas player without the tedium of residential qualification. There was an immediate scramble to sign Garry Sobers, the world's greatest all-rounder, who was still at the peak of his powers. Seven counties entertained hopes of success, few with more determination or reasons for hope than Lancashire. So generous, in their own eyes, was the offer made to Sobers that Cedric Rhoades felt that, were it be turned down, 'the Club should publish exactly what he had asked for'.

After weeks of indecision, news came through that Nottinghamshire had outbid Lancashire. Was the leading sports agent of the day, Bagenal Harvey, to blame for Sobers' decision to go where the money was best? Smarting under the rejection, it was resolved at Old Trafford that in future the committee would not deal with agents. But, with no Sobers, the Club had no obvious Plan B. The hope was still to secure the services of a proven leader or a big name. There was another fruitless approach to Alan Smith and a concerted effort was made to bring Bob Barber back to Lancashire.

Barber had already made clear to Warwickshire that he was now eyeing a business career and would be retiring from first-class cricket. He would, in any case, have been wary about returning: 'I was not prepared to repeat what had been a very unhappy experience.' Everything was different now, he was assured by the chairman's emissary Arthur Booth, the former Yorkshire spin bowler, who was now a tireless worker for the Red Rose cause. Refusing to take no for an answer, Booth pleaded for a further chance to persuade the former captain to return.

'Arthur asked to come and see me. He stayed as a family friend overnight. He said the club were desperate and had nobody.' Bob Barber listened to Booth's entreaty and then told him that the man for whom Lancashire were searching was already at Old Trafford. 'I told him they were crazy! That in my view Jackie would be ideal for putting the club back on the rails if they really wanted that. I believe at the time we spoke there was a risk that he would not be retained! Crazy people!'

What was it that prompted Barber to champion Jack's cause as skipper? Though the governance of the club was improving, he felt there had long been a lack of integrity around Old Trafford, with its history of internecine feuding in committee. 'People of integrity had to step up to the plate. Jack had integrity. He was a good enough player to lead from the front on the field and a man of sufficient principle to set an example off the field.'

February arrived with no decision made when Jack took a call from Jack Wood, Secretary at Old Trafford. 'We've just had a committee meeting and they want you to take the captaincy on a caretaker basis while they look for somebody else,' he was told. There had been few previous hints. 'Of course I was overjoyed,' Jack now says. 'Whether it was for one month or two months, it was a great privilege to be captain of your county. I mean ... the chance of playing for England and things like that had long since gone, so that was the ultimate aim.'

Jack turned to Florence to share his elation. 'And what do you think she said? She said, "You'll have to have all your teeth out." I said, "What do you mean?" At the time I had about three or four at the top and about five at the bottom – they were ready to come out. She said, "Well you can't be doing television interviews with teeth like that!"' But the media could not wait for a dental appointment. 'By the time I'd got all my new teeth, I'd done all my television interviews. But I still suffered all the pain.'

With hindsight Jack was the logical short-term answer to Lancashire's distress call. Yet Jack Wood's call had come as a surprise. 'When I look back maybe I shouldn't have been quite so surprised. But, having been on the staff since 1955, you learn a bit about the workings of the club, the committee and the way they think, how people's hopes are built up and the next minute they're dashed.'

Jack had led the side half a dozen times during the previous summer. Of those who might at one time have been serious alternatives, David Green, hampered by a leg injury, had experienced another disappointing year and had been sacked, moving on to Gloucestershire, where he was to become one of *Wisden's* five Cricketers of the Year after his first season. Geoff Pullar's star remained in decline, while Duncan Worsley, captain of Oxford University in 1964, who had also led Lancashire's second eleven, had played no part in the second half of the season, a shoulder injury hastening his retirement into the teaching profession.

Jack brought to the task the experience of 13 years on the Lancashire staff, an acute and observant cricketing brain and universal popularity among the players. Whilst never keen to hog the limelight, he was not one to shy away from responsibility and he relished the challenge of leadership. Over the years he had seen so much go wrong: the aloof Cyril Washbrook letting situations drift; the enforced distancing of the young Bob Barber from the men he was supposed to lead; the hapless Joe Blackledge with the odds stacked against him; the disunity when Ken Grieves' time in charge had ended with wholesale sackings; the iconic Brian Statham with no appetite for making tough decisions and an autopilot attitude to directing affairs on the field.

Geoff Edrich:
'a model skipper'.

But, from his second eleven days, Jack had also seen Geoff Edrich at close quarters, and he knew that here was his model for skippering Lancashire. Many years later Edrich would return to Old Trafford for a former players' reunion. Walking with difficulty, he entered the room to all-round applause. This was the measure of a man who had been so widely admired in his playing days, not so much for his weight of runs or his leg trap catches as his indomitable spirit. 'Everybody would do anything for Geoff,' says Jack. 'You'd sweat your guts out for Geoff,' says Roy Tattersall, as he remembers his inspirational leadership in 1956, always encouraging and happy to make suggestions but never dictating.

Jack remembered Edrich's influence off the field with his young charges in the second eleven: how they would go back to the hotel and talk about the day's play and discuss the strengths and weaknesses of the opposing batsmen or the way to play their best bowlers. 'Geoff would talk cricket day in, day out, night in, night out. About half past nine you'd probably go out for a curry or fish and chips, then to bed. But Geoff'd stay up till the early hours of the morning. He'd stay up all night with anybody to talk cricket.'

When Geoff Edrich left Old Trafford, carrying the can for some high-spirited behaviour from his second team, it was yet another sad and needless ending of a loyal career. And it meant the departure of a man who influenced Jack's appreciation of the game's more subtle twists. Cricket is a 'situations game', Jack believes. 'You get situations that repeat themselves time and again over the years. The secret is to recognize them when they occur, and hopefully you've got the people in your side to deal with them.' Edrich was always a positive captain, and Jack followed him in abhorring games that were allowed to drift, as if the only objective was getting the day over and into the bar.

When Jack took up the reins, there were a few seasoned professionals on whom he could still call, but all would soon move on and he feels he was lucky to have taken on a mainly young side with players most of whom he knew well. 'When I took over as captain, a lot of the players had only one way to look and that was towards me. As senior pro I'd been on the staff a long time and a lot of them were young lads I'd brought up through the second eleven in the previous three years. So if I said something, they virtually took it as gospel.'

All this was a far cry from the problems Bob Barber had faced and which had characterised Lancashire's cricket in the early sixties, when the 'heavy brigade' had held sway. Jack recalls the unhealthy attitude: 'If you get a very unsuccessful side, though it may have talented players in it, the next best thing for some of the players, if they haven't had too good a day on the field, is to make sure they have a good night off it, especially when playing away from home, where they can get away with it.'

Could Jack have risen to the challenge if this had been the dominant culture of the team he inherited? He finds it difficult to see how he could have tackled anything differently, albeit he would not have had the extra burden of the anti-university feeling and resentment of the amateur that Bob Barber faced. 'I would have found it a lot more difficult and stressful than when I did take over,' he says.

Determined that he would banish all traces of the cynical and selfish attitudes of the early sixties, Jack vowed that his team must start enjoying playing the game. Then the crowd would enjoy watching them. A positive team spirit had to be restored with players happy for each others' successes. It was a far cry from the times when there had been dressing-room chuckles at the failures of Cyril Washbrook or plotting for the young Bob Bennett to fail. 'If it had gone wrong because I made a wrong decision at the toss, then there were ten people trying to put it right. I honestly believe that was because of the way I'd looked after them and helped them along the road in earlier seasons.'

With David Lloyd and Barry Wood, soon to be joined by Frank Hayes, as batsmen; Peter Lever, as the away swing bowler which Jack always liked to have in a team; and Ken Shuttleworth, held back only by a lack of belief in his own talent – there were five players destined to play for England. And there was one other youngster who Jack feels deserved it just as much, Harry Pilling. Also in the fourteen from whom the side was invariably picked was 'a man who would die for you,' John Sullivan. 'It was great to have people like John in the side. When you said, "Unfortunately you're left out," and he'd say, "I'm quite happy to leave it up to Jack Bond and Lancashire to pick me to play when they want me to play." He probably wanted to play in every match but he realised he couldn't, and when he was picked he was overjoyed. Other lads would sulk and go into their shell and probably wouldn't talk to you, avoid you if they could.'

For this first summer Brian Statham was still available to lead the attack with Ken Higgs, while there would be two more seasons of Graham Atkinson and one for the veteran John Savage, who was to be a steadying hand in the attack and provide the ideal foil for yet another youngster, 21-year-old David Hughes. 'John played a big part in the development of David Hughes in that particular year because I was able to bowl the experienced spinner at one end and the young slow left-armer at the other, knowing that John would be economical. And if you've got an off-spinner and a slow left-armer, you can try and make sure they're bowling to the batsman you want them to bowl at.'

The final piece in the jigsaw was a new wicket-keeper. While Keith Goodwin would continue to serve Lancashire loyally and well, the recruitment of Farokh Engineer (as their overseas player) gave the county an international keeper and a dashing bat whose runs would be made with panache. Soon he would become as true a Lancastrian as those born in Bolton or Rochdale. Engineer had made his first visit to England with the Indian tourists the previous summer. He recalls the match that had been hurriedly switched to Southport, when he had 'given it a whack' at the top of the order, only to discover on returning to the pavilion that the bowler he had carted over the railway line had been Brian Statham, one of his childhood heroes. His enterprising approach made him an attractive proposition to several counties, but he chose Lancashire because he knew of the friendliness of the Lancashire people. It was a signing for which Jack would always be grateful, seldom making a tactical move without consulting his wicket-keeper, while for Farokh there was to be a first summer in which he would learn of the many pubs that would still be open for 'one last nightcap' as his one-time hero, Brian Statham, motored him around the country.

Farokh Engineer,
'keeping with panache'.

If salt needed to be rubbed into Lancashire's wounds with their failure to bring Garry Sobers to Old Trafford, it was soon to be applied. The first match of the new season took Jack's team to Trent Bridge in late April for the first round of the Gillette Cup. Lancashire batted first and Sobers gained an immediate lbw decision against Wood and, with Atkinson making a duck, Lancashire were 3 for two. Thanks to 61 from Sullivan, they reached 166 and, with three Notts men out for 51, it seemed that this modest total might be enough. But Sobers now took command with the bat, his undefeated 75 ensuring a comfortable four-wicket win. Jack remembers playing on in rain and appalling light. 'I thought if we can't get him out in the dark, what chance have we got in daylight?'

This early reverse set the pattern for the first few championship matches. Lancashire's programme began at Canterbury where a low scoring game in which batting became gradually easier saw the home side victorious by six wickets. Then followed a string of rain-affected draws, after which Lancashire came within a whisker of victory at Lord's as Brian Statham, with six for 48 in the second innings, strove vainly for the final Middlesex wicket.

Jack looks back on the Middlesex match with wry humour. He had declared the Lancashire innings closed at lunchtime on the final day, setting Middlesex 267 to win. At least he thought he had declared! 'At lunch Fred Titmus was sat next to me and I declared to him then. So we walked down through the Long Room at the bell and, lo and behold, coming through the other door was Middlesex as well. So there's 22 of us in the Long Room. Fred said, "What's going on?" I said, "I declared." He said, "When did you declare?" I said, "I declared when we were having lunch." He said, "Well it must have been my deaf ear!"'

By this time the umpires were standing in the middle awaiting the players, so Jack called them back and explained the situation. 'They said, "Right, Fred, what roller do you want?" We were 20 minutes late starting after lunch. And, of course, we had declared hoping to get a result.' Had Jack been sitting the other side of Titmus at lunch, there might have been an extra ten points for Lancashire.

Earlier in the same match Geoff Pullar had revived memories of the glory years with what was to be his final century for Lancashire. Thereafter his form dipped, and by mid-season he was out of the team. The following summer he was playing alongside Green for Gloucestershire. To Jack, Pullar will always remain an enigmatic cricketer. 'We used to call him Noddy. He loved reading Westerns. He'd be reading before he went in to bat, and he'd sleep before he went in. He never watched the game. I remember him getting a hundred at Lord's between lunch and tea. He had batted all morning for 29 then he let loose. A brilliant player, great to watch! Yet there was something about the game he didn't like. I think it was particularly fielding. He'd had knee problems and his flat feet kept him out of National Service. Yet he could play for Lancashire – it seemed strange.'

'I remember he got a hundred against Worcestershire. I batted for a while, didn't get very many then I got out. But Geoff wanted a runner, so there's me still having my pads on. I didn't even come up the steps and I ran for Geoff. He was probably 30-odd and everything was fine until he got to 99. And when he was 99 he hit it and he beat me to the other end. I'm not joking, I'm at square leg and I'm running, and I look up and he's at the bowling end before me! And Don Kenyon is stood there with the ball over the bails. And he said, "What are you doing here?" Geoff said, "I'm sorry. I got very excited." He said, "Well b ... off back to that other end." But he let him get a hundred. A lot of people who knew Don Kenyon would think that a bit strange, because he wasn't the sort of man to give an inch to anyone.'

Jack's misfortune in sitting on the wrong side of Titmus at Lord's having cost Lancashire dearly, there was another chance to break their championship duck at Old Trafford, but this time they were thwarted by Vanburn Holder in their efforts to score 199 in three hours to beat Worcestershire. This 48-run loss was followed by a heavy defeat at the hands of Yorkshire that consigned the team to the bottom of the Championship. 'What can one say about Lancashire?' wrote John Kay in the *Manchester Evening News*. 'Nothing except to remark that they fielded superbly when the heat was on yesterday and bowled unsparingly. But until their brittle batsmen find form the side will struggle.'

There were draws against Derbyshire and Cambridge University. Then, in mid-June, came the season's first victory, against Middlesex at Old Trafford. There was a bizarre twist to Middlesex's first innings. Statham and Higgs had opened the bowling; then Jack brought on Shuttleworth as first change. 'I must have thought I had him on at the wrong end, so I took Shuttleworth off and I bowled Woody at that end. And straightaway he got a wicket. Some people, even if he'd got a wicket, would have taken him off and still put the other bowler on, but I kept Woody on and he kept chipping in with a wicket. So what do you do? He wouldn't have let me take him off!' Barry Wood's final figures were 19-6-52-7, the best of his career.

Seventies from Pullar and Pilling gave Lancashire a lead of 51 on first innings and, when the pace men bowled the visitors out a second time for 185, the target was 135 in just under two hours. Jack came in at 47 for four. Soon it was 80 for five but, partnered by David Lloyd for most of the way, he saw his side home with five deliveries to spare. His undefeated 35 was top score and set a pattern whereby, in tight situations when runs were needed for victory, it was invariably the skipper who led the side past the winning post. Forty years may have passed, but Jack still cherishes the memory of this first elusive victory: 'It was Ken Shuttleworth in at the end. He hit the winning run, a tickle down the leg side.'

It would be some time before Lancashire could celebrate victory again, and Jack's next mission was a rearguard action to stave off defeat in a rain-affected match against Kent. From 10 for five in their second innings, with help from Lloyd and Engineer, Jack steered the ship to safety. Another four draws, inclement weather invariably playing a part, preceded the next success, another tight, low-scoring match, this time against Sussex at Eastbourne. Successive scores read: Sussex 80; Lancashire 88; Sussex 78. It was a field day for the faster bowlers, of whom none fared better than Allan Jones, in later years a first-class umpire, but now playing in only his second county match, who took eight for 25 in the first innings.

Yet, with Lancashire needing 71 to win, he was to become the villain of the piece and Jack the hero. 'This total was reached,' *Wisden* recorded, 'only through sensible batting by the captain, Bond, and two dropped catches. Both fielding lapses were by Jones. He misjudged the first catch at mid-off when Bond was 23, and off the second ball of the last over he put down a return offered by Statham.' Victory came with two wickets and three balls to spare, Jack finishing with 32 not out.

Jack looks back on the kind of match that is no longer seen by the spectator at today's first-class game. 'There's no way you'd have had a result like that if it hadn't been a rain-affected pitch. Allan

Jones just kept on hitting this spot on a length. It was evil, to be honest. It made batting very interesting and it made for an interesting game. It brings out character in people, I think, playing in adverse conditions.'

A loss to Nottinghamshire was now followed by a string of victories. Derbyshire went down by 124 runs, and Warwickshire were overwhelmed at Edgbaston by 188 runs, Jack scoring 42 not out and 48. Then, after a Lancashire League XI had also been beaten, Northamptonshire and then Somerset succumbed. The Northants match was notable for Jack's decision to close Lancashire's first innings when within sight of his first century since 1965. He was on 93 when Lancashire, with eight wickets down, were 61 ahead as stumps approached on the second day. Jack's preference to attack the Northants batsmen for half an hour was rewarded with three wickets before the close and a ten-wicket victory before lunch the next day. 'That's the way I'd been brought up to play the game by people like Geoff Edrich,' he says. 'Mind you, we won with half a day to spare so it makes you wonder. Perhaps I could have got my hundred with no trouble and still won the game, but the thought of them having to bat for half an hour when they'd been fielding all day – you can't miss that opportunity.'

At Weston-super-Mare the margin of victory against Somerset was just eleven runs, David Hughes making his mark with six for 61 as a target of only 123 proved beyond the home batsmen. This was the kind of win that comes for a team on a roll and it meant that Lancashire went into the Roses game at Old Trafford in good heart. This had long been earmarked as the farewell match for Brian Statham, his 430th for Lancashire, and it was also Ken Higgs' benefit. A rampant Statham sent Red Rose supporters home in high spirits as Yorkshire, replying to Lancashire's 162, stood at 34 for eight on the first evening. Their innings closed next day for 61, but in the end the game was nicely poised with Yorkshire still requiring 64 with five wickets intact.

To Jack, this draw matched some of the wins over weaker sides. 'We used to get beaten by Yorkshire regularly, so to come away with a draw was quite good for us.' Glamorgan, destined to become champions the next year, were enjoying a fine season and now inflicted two defeats on Lancashire. There was an innings victory at Old Trafford, but two sporting declarations in the return match at Cardiff set up a nail biter before Jack's men were beaten by four wickets. Jack recalls the pressure as he calculated the moment to bring the Lancashire innings to a close, with the Glamorgan secretary and former captain pacing up and down. 'Wilf Wooller was prowling along that top balcony where the two dressing rooms were, chuntering and muttering and saying, "You're killing the game, Lancashire. You should have declared twenty minutes ago."' Jack eventually set Glamorgan 178 in 130 minutes, a target that the Welsh side reached thanks to a superbly paced 95 not out by Alan Jones.

There were two more draws before the season ended on a high note, with a pair of wins at Old Trafford. First Gloucestershire were defeated by four wickets with three balls left, Jack once again at the crease on 38 having made a useful 35 in the first innings. Then his 44 helped to build a substantial first innings lead before Essex were comfortably beaten by nine wickets. Just five runs were needed to secure the win. The pages of *Wisden* reveal that the wicket to fall was that of Peter Lever. It brings a smile to Jack's face: 'That's typical Peter. "I'll go in and knock them off." I suppose he hadn't taken too many wickets!'

There had been eight wins in the Championship against six losses. Lancashire's strong finish had lifted them to sixth place in the table, the highest for eight years. Jack now looks back and remembers how apprehensive he had been at the outset. 'You're bound to be aren't you? A new captain, a side that's not been doing too well for a few years. It was an exciting time, but everybody was a little bit nervous at the start.' The initial objective had been to avoid losing. 'What I wanted to do in my captaincy early on was to try to get us to draw games initially. Because we had got into the habit of losing – I'm not saying not caring about losing – but you get into a habit and we had lost a lot of games over four or five years. If you can't win, you make damn sure you don't lose – that was the attitude I wanted to instil in them, the same attitude that we'd had in the second eleven.'

Then the wins had come. 'Gradually the last five or six games of the season the dressing room was unbelievable. There was a real buzz about it and an excitement and a real feeling of team spirit, and everybody wanting everybody else in the side to do well.'

It was a notable season too in other ways. For the first time there had there been no points for a first innings lead. Instead, bonus points had been introduced for runs made and wickets taken in the first 85 overs of the first innings. A maximum of five were available to the bowlers, but there was no limit for batsmen, who earned a point for every 25 runs above 150. Yet, in another damp summer, there had not been a glut of runs with the championship average at 23.53. Lancashire's relative strength in bowling had given the county its edge, their average of 18.93 bettered only by Yorkshire; but the batsmen had averaged just 19.56, the lowest return of all the counties. Barely credibly, with 26.60, Jack headed the Lancashire averages. Whatever the figures, his runs had often been made when the chips were down. Moreover, as *Wisden* noted, he had 'frequently sacrificed his wicket attempting to speed things up.' His reputation as a fighter in a tight corner had been reinforced and his powers of leadership were now manifest for all to see.

Chapter Eight

'And there was this new competition'

When the Lancashire players assembled for the start of the 1969 season they no longer had a caretaker captain. The decision to re-appoint Jack Bond had been unanimous in the cricket committee. Meanwhile, without Statham and Pullar and with Savage moving into a coaching role, the side increasingly bore the hallmark of its captain. The mood was upbeat. 'We were expecting everything would be all rosy and we'd climb even further up the County Championship,' Jack says. 'We were obviously looking to do better in the Gillette. And there was this new competition.'

This new competition! In 1969, spurred on by the interest aroused by televised Sunday matches played by the Rothmans International Cavaliers, the TCCB had devised a 40-over competition for the counties. Branded in its first year as the John Player's County League, but soon to become the John Player League and be widely known as the JPL, it was also to be played on Sundays. As with the Gillette in its early days, and later with Twenty20 cricket, there were many counties who raised little enthusiasm for a game so far removed from their customary first-class fare. Jack remembers Brian Close saying that 'it wasn't a proper game of cricket' and that senior players in some of the counties preferred to have Sunday off rather than have to play. But Jack saw it differently: 'We had three chances to win a trophy.'

It would not be long before Lancashire's chances had receded in two of the competitions. The championship programme began with a string of draws – 21 of Lancashire's 24 matches in 1969 were drawn – and hopes in the Gillette evaporated at the first hurdle in early June as Yorkshire cruised to victory by seven wickets at Old Trafford. 'So the whole season revolved around the new competition,' Jack recalls, adding that 'it wasn't intended that way at all.'

The defeat by Yorkshire was not for want of planning. The small selection committee had identified the principal danger. 'It was all about how to get John Hampshire out,' Jack remembers. 'Get him out and you've won the game.' The Lancashire openers made a very slow start and the later batsmen did well to reach 173 for eight. When Yorkshire batted, the challenge posed by Hampshire was not as foreseen. 'Our problem was getting him in!' Jack chuckles. The score had reached 138 before the danger man came to the wicket, and by this time it was plain sailing for Yorkshire.

Over the years the shorter timescales of the limited-overs game have rewarded sides, sometimes of limited class and experience, who have put a premium on disciplined bowling backed up by energy and enthusiasm in the field. So it was with Lancashire, where the young team were quick to embrace the John Player League. 'A lot of the youngsters had been brought up on league cricket, one-day cricket. They seemed to adapt very quickly to it. And we had a lot of very positive cricketers in the side,' Jack says.

Jack Simmons,
at 28 'an important addition'.

An important addition was 28-year-old Jack Simmons, an off-spinner with a famously flat trajectory, who came into the side as the replacement for Savage. Waiting until he had completed his training as a draughtsman before signing a contract with Lancashire, Simmons' arrival was timely. He joined as the one-day game was putting a premium on the value of a reliable containing bowler. 'I came on the scene at the right time,' he acknowledges. 'If I had gone five years earlier, unless I'd have changed my trajectory drastically to be someone like a John Savage, I'd probably have played in the second team and not been given another contract after two years.'

Simmons would extend his career until the age of 48 and later become chairman of the club. To his captain, Simmons always exemplified the values he sought in his players: 'Whether he thought you were right or wrong, he would do what you asked him to. The only thing with Jack he was not such a good timekeeper.

He'd come in late, which would aggravate me, but he'd always have an excuse – he'd come in with a bacon sandwich in his mouth and you knew where he'd been – to the shop down the road on his way in for a bacon butty.' With his legendary fondness for pies, Simmons soon became a great favourite with the Lancashire crowds. 'He looked a bit too big and a bit bulky at times to be playing county cricket,' says his captain, 'but people love players like that, don't they?'

This was also the year in which Clive Lloyd was first qualified to play competitive cricket for Lancashire. His batting and fielding had made a big impression on Farokh Engineer when the West Indians had toured India and Farokh recommended him to the county. 'But he wears glasses,' Cyril Washbrook had protested. Fortunately any deficiencies with Lloyd's eyesight were ignored and his long and happy association with Lancashire began. However, with the West Indies team touring in the first half of the summer, his appearances were restricted to just nine championship matches and he was able to play little part in the Sunday league. Lloyd nevertheless played a crucial role in starting the county's John Player season on the right foot, an undefeated 59 steering Lancashire to a five-wicket win against Sussex at Hove.

Lloyd did not return to the county side until the end of July, and in his absence the match against Essex at Chelmsford was lost by 108 runs. The home side's 265 for six was to remain the highest total recorded in this first season of the 40-over competition. As the years passed new scoring peaks were achieved and new norms set, but in the early years of the John Player League such a target was of Himalayan proportions. Once early wickets had been lost, Lancashire faced inevitable defeat. Yet Jack looks back at what he learned from this match as crucial to his strategy for the rest of the season.

The Essex batsmen had hit with great freedom towards the end of the innings, Keith Boyce reaching 50 in 23 minutes, and one bowler, John Sullivan, had suffered a fearful pummelling, ending with figures of 8-0-73-1. 'I realised then that you have got to have more than five bowlers. You need to have a relief column coming up.' With Clive Lloyd away and Barry Wood not playing – 'I think he'd been taking down a shed and it fell on him' – there had been no-one to whom Jack had felt he could turn. It would not happen again.

The first Sunday match at Old Trafford brought a comfortable win against Nottinghamshire, now deprived of Sobers. Then, in a match at Bristol truncated by rain, the winning run came from Jack's bat in the final over to bring a third win in four matches. The next Sunday brought a still undefeated Surrey to Old Trafford. When Jack was fourth out with the score on 12, only a battling 60 from Harry Pilling enabled Lancashire to reach a barely defendable 130. But Surrey started almost as shakily as Lancashire, and with John Edrich, Micky Stewart and Younis Ahmed mustering one run between them, the score was 16 for three. Opener Mike Edwards then led a recovery. It was slow progress, but by the last over the league leaders had reached 126 for eight with Arnold Long and Geoff Arnold at the crease.

First Arnold was run out. There was an ironic touch as the man to replace him was Jim Cumbes, who had transferred to Surrey on Jack's advice, his way as a pace bowler at Lancashire blocked by Higgs, Lever and Shuttleworth. 'It was my first Sunday league game,' he now recalls. 'I was tempted to take a quick single and got sent back and I slipped in the middle of the wicket. I was on my hands and knees when the wicket was broken.'

'That will be my everlasting picture of you in my mind – on all fours,' Jack quipped as they all returned to the pavilion with Lancashire the fortunate winners by four runs, their closest call of the campaign. 'To get two run outs like that with Arnold Long at the other end! I seem to remember him being quite upset about it,' Jack now recalls. 'If we'd lost that game it might have thrown a different complexion on things, but I doubt it!'

Lancashire, on the brink of 'won 3, lost 2' when Shuttleworth had begun his final over against Surrey, now had a season's record of four victories to one defeat. Winning was soon to become a habit, successive match results reading:

1 June	Old Trafford	Derbyshire	Won by five wickets
15 June	Peterborough	Northants	Won by six wickets
26 June	Blackheath	Kent	Won by 20 runs
6 July	Old Trafford	Somerset	Won by four wickets
13 July	Southport	Glamorgan	Won by nine wickets
27 July	Old Trafford	Middlesex	Won by six wickets

Jack now had a clear plan of attack and he found his bowlers responding week after week. 'It wasn't important just to keep the runs down. It was important to take wickets. For a good number of overs we set attacking fields, encouraging the bowlers to pitch the ball up as well, so we had the chance of bowling people out when they were hitting across the line. And the fielding became very important. Some of the catches and run outs and ground fielding – it was tremendous.'

This was the hallmark of Jack's leadership, the trait that had been noticeable even in the difficult early matches of the previous summer. A man whose fielding had often helped to secure his place in the side in his younger days never lost his enthusiasm for this side of the game. 'We enjoyed fielding. It wasn't a case of getting the two and a half hours' fielding over and then start batting – it was a real enjoyment to go and field.'

There was no play on 3 August in the scheduled match with Yorkshire at Old Trafford, but it was business as usual at Leicester with a 65-run victory on 10 August. Essex, the only side to have beaten Lancashire, had been hot on their heels all summer, but on this same Sunday they had lost to Surrey at Leyton. After this round of matches the top of the table read:

	Played	Won	Tied	Lost	N/R	Points
Lancashire	13	11	0	1	1	45
Essex	13	9	0	3	1	37
Surrey	13	9	0	3	1	37
Hampshire	12	9	0	3	0	36

Only three counties had a mathematical chance of overhauling Lancashire. While Surrey had dealt a blow to Essex's chances, Hampshire had won four matches in a row, including a dramatic one-run defeat of Leicestershire when they had achieved a run out on the final ball. With a game in hand on the other front runners, their next match was at Old Trafford.

The Lancashire team was beginning to attract the enthusiastic and vocal crowds hitherto associated with the other Old Trafford, but Sunday cricket was also becoming a family day out. For the visit of Hampshire there were 12,000 in the ground, more than paid to watch all eight of Worcestershire's home matches in the league that summer. For Lancashire, victory would mean that the title was virtually guaranteed, with Essex or Surrey needing a miraculously increased run rate to make a challenge.

Hopes that Lancashire might be crowned in front of their home supporters perished as their batsmen fell 48 short of Hampshire's

174 for seven. Only Sullivan, with more than half Lancashire's runs from his own bat, made much impression as Derek Shackleton and Butch White conceded only 21 runs in the 14 overs they bowled. This was the chance for Lancashire's rivals to close the gap, but Essex lost to Warwickshire, and Surrey, who were to lose their last three matches, were trounced by Middlesex at Lord's. So, with Lancashire's hopes now resting on their match with Warwickshire at Nuneaton, Hampshire had become the side best placed to overtake them.

A week later it was Sullivan again. His fourth-wicket partnership of 105 with Clive Lloyd ensured a challenging total of 204 for five, to which Warwickshire could muster only 153 in reply. News that Hampshire had gone down to Essex meant that Lancashire were the first county to lift the John Player trophy and take with it a cheque for £1,000. It wasn't how Jack had planned the season, but he was carried along with the euphoria. 'From playing in front of a couple of thousand in a championship match, suddenly the ground became alive. Not just at Old Trafford but wherever we played away from home we got a good following. Mind you, I've always believed that any form of cricket should be a spectator sport – you're not playing the game for the players' benefit, you're playing it for the people watching. But it's surprising – it does bring more out of you. It creates more pressure, but it gets the best out of you as well.'

Lancashire's final Sunday match of the season took them to Worcester as champions. No longer was there the pressure to win, so the team took the opportunity to pitch for one of the individual prizes on offer. To spice up the competition, prizes had been offered for sixes – 355 were hit altogether, each one worth £2 16s 4d (£2.82) – and for taking four wickets in a match. There was one other prize for the season's fastest fifty, measured in those days in the old currency of minutes rather than balls. The front runner for this award was Keith Boyce – for his innings against Lancashire in early May – and it was his opponents that day who now planned to deprive him. After Worcestershire had batted first and scored a useful 158, the target for Lancashire's batsmen was to reach fifty in less than 23 minutes. David Lloyd was designated as the man to bat quietly through while the others threw their bats at the ball. It didn't work. In the end Lancashire did not even score quickly enough to win the match and Lloyd, whose sacrificial role brought him an undefeated 64 at the end of 40 overs, was regarded (by those not in the know) as the man who had played for himself!

Formalities neatly observed.

For the traditionalists around Old Trafford, one-day success was little compensation for a poor performance in the Championship. Sixth place in 1968 had proved a false dawn as Lancashire slid back to fifteenth in the table. Yet they were not an easy team to beat, suffering just one defeat – to Derbyshire at Blackpool, where the batsmen failed by 16 runs to reach a target of 148. By comparison, second-placed Gloucestershire lost six times. Despite another damp summer the batsmen earned more bonus points but, with no Statham and with Higgs and Shuttleworth slipping back from outstandingly good years, the bowlers, responsible for 105 points the previous year, now brought in only 39. With no points awarded for a draw, Lancashire owed their lowly position to managing just two victories all summer, against the bottom county Somerset and over Middlesex at Lord's, where victory came by 14 runs off the last available ball.

The Lord's game was a match dominated by pace bowlers, with the Australian Alan Connolly principally responsible for dismissing Lancashire for 91, in which Jack, with 31 not out, was one of only two batsmen to reach double figures. There were six cheap wickets for Higgs as Middlesex could do no more than draw level. David Lloyd and Graham Atkinson, playing only championship matches in his final year, then laid a painstaking platform at the start of Lancashire's second innings as the batsmen ground their way to 173. Caution remained the watchword as Middlesex sought 174 for victory.

Graham Barlow, later to play three Tests for England but now a 19-year-old taking part in his first championship match, was batting at number six. He had watched the last of the established batsmen depart and continued to play patiently as Lancashire worked their way through his tail-end partners. By the time Lever prepared to bowl the final over, his thirtieth of the innings, Barlow had been joined by last man Connolly.

'We got it wrong in the last over,' Jack now relates. 'We'd got Graham Barlow facing the last over when they'd got nine down. Peter Lever was bowling to him, and he'd bowled all afternoon. He bowled five balls and we couldn't get him out. Then, in desperation, he bowled a bouncer – the very last ball of the game. Graham Barlow, God bless him, shouldered arms and it hit him and dropped straight onto the stumps. He'd played magnificently. We were all highly delighted, but I can honestly say I was sorry for Graham.'

There was to be a sequel. Sir Neville Cardus, soon to be Lancashire's president, knocked on the dressing-room door and asked for the captain. Sir Neville was invited in. 'We were stood there in this big room. There's Peter Lever and myself and Farokh Engineer and Neville Cardus. And he said, "I just wanted to say that was a magnificent piece of bowling, the best I've seen in a decade, Peter. Aren't you proud to be a Lancastrian?" Peter looked at me and he looked at him, and he said, "I'm sorry, Sir Neville, I was born in Todmorden on the Yorkshire side." And Farokh said, "These bloody foreigners!"'

Chapter Nine

'They stormed the gates to get in'

The elation of winning the new John Player League could not conceal Jack's disappointment at slipping back in the Championship. 'The County Championship is the one where you feel as if you've really achieved something. The season would have been really horrendous if we had lost, say, six games, but the mere fact that we'd only lost once – at least we came away from the season with a bit of pride because of it. But we were so disappointed because we had done so well in the County Championship the season before.'

That winter Jack prepared for his benefit. A decade later the professionally organised six-figure benefit would become commonplace for those who played for a major county; but in 1970 it was all more homespun. Jack went round the pubs with bats to be raffled, spending as much on drinks in some places as he took for the fund, but he never attended the meetings of his benefit committee. 'I probably made the mistake of not paying enough attention to my benefit that year because I was the captain and I was so involved in what was going on, on the field,' he says. About £2,000 was taken at his chosen match, the championship fixture against Yorkshire, and his final cheque was for £7,230 17s 4d. 'It was still a decent sum,' he feels. 'It represented a lot of work by a lot of people, and it was very much appreciated.'

As he prepared for the new season, Jack was determined that there would be improvements. He had good reason for optimism. There was a vibrant air in the dressing room: he had a young and enthusiastic team and, for the first time, they could look forward to a full season with Clive Lloyd in their ranks. Not 26 until mid-summer, Lloyd was approaching the peak of his ability. As a batsman few could match the range and power of his left-handed strokes, while as a lurking presence in the covers his name was linked with the South African Colin Bland as the best fielder in the world. Moreover, Lloyd was a bowler to whom his captain would soon be turning when in need of a wicket. A contract dispute had taken Higgs, the last of the old guard, into league cricket at Blackpool, placing a greater burden on Lever and Shuttleworth. So it was often Lloyd who would step into the breach if either was away.

To some outsiders it was a surprise that a West Indian and an Indian could blend so happily into a county dressing room. They did not know Clive Lloyd and Farokh Engineer! Lloyd had already experienced the warmth of Lancashire hospitality when he had signed as professional with Haslingden in the Lancashire League. A black man stood out on the streets of the town, but he says, 'I have always felt comfortable in Lancashire, because I was always made to feel welcome. I was treated so well.' So it would be when he arrived at Old Trafford, where he immediately warmed to Jack's style of captaincy and the dressing-room humour. 'And Florence was lovely,' he says. 'She used to wash all my underwear, and there aren't many county captains' wives you can say that about.'

It was business as usual as the season began at Old Trafford with an eight-wicket victory over Middlesex in the John Player League, but this year there was a more encouraging start for the older members – a championship win against Leicestershire at Old Trafford, in which Jack played an important part. With Lancashire needing 165, the match was in the balance at 71 for four when he came in, but his 42 in an unbroken partnership with Engineer steered the county home by six wickets on the second evening.

Leicestershire had also capitulated in the Sunday game by 92 runs, so the campaign had started well on two fronts. Later that week the team set off for Kent, where a championship match began on the Saturday at Dartford before the teams moved to Beckenham for a Sunday league match that was to end in controversy. With rain around, the match had been reduced to 35 overs, from which Lancashire, helped by a breezy 32 from Jack, scored 202 for seven. Soon after the Kent innings began 'in Stygian gloom and under threatening skies,' the rain began to fall more steadily. 'We could have come off after three or four overs,' Jack reckons, but the Lancashire players stayed on until, at the end of the ninth over and with the score on 58 for one, they were surprised to see the batsmen heading triumphantly for the pavilion, leaving fielders and umpires in the middle, the rain now falling steadily.

In the early days of the competition, before the brilliantly conceived but unfathomable mystery of the Duckworth-Lewis formula, all that was required of the side batting second in a shortened match was to score more than their opponents had managed in the same number of overs. Invariably this made life hard for the team with runs on the board, and it now worked to Kent's advantage as they maintained that they had only to pass 57 in ten overs, the minimum number required for a valid contest. But no-one had advised Jack of any limit being imposed on the Kent innings. Had he known, he might have come off earlier, while it could also be argued that Kent had not batted the mandatory ten overs.

Kent captain Colin Cowdrey claimed that the umpires had confirmed a Kent win, but a call was made to Lord's and a ruling came back that it was 'only provisional'. 'If Lancashire appeal, as they are expected to do,' wrote John Woodcock in *The Times*, 'they will have a case, technical though it may be.' Next day, back at Dartford, there was a meeting behind the hessian screen that served to create the umpires' quarters, between the officials and the two captains, with the Kent side strengthened by the presence of their former captain David Clark, now a member of the MCC committee.

Jack was assured that there would be a meeting at Lord's later in the week, at which he would be allowed to put his case. But the promised meeting never took place. Before the team returned to Old Trafford, a letter had been received confirming the Kent win. Whatever the merits of the case, Jack still fulminates at the injustice. 'Cowdrey and David Clark were both well connected at Lord's. It was a case of the establishment looking after its own.'

On the field, the Dartford pitch thwarted both sets of bowlers, a draw bringing Lancashire eleven points but also providing a stage for the full majesty of Clive Lloyd's stroke play as he reached his century from 90 balls on his way to 163. Innings of this kind helped to make Lancashire the fastest-scoring side in the Championship, their runs coming at 54.64 per hundred balls against 43.14 the previous year.

The annual sortie to Liverpool brought a second championship win in three matches as Northants were defeated by nine wickets. So the Lancashire players set off in good heart for their meeting with Yorkshire at Headingley. Making the most of a good batting pitch, Barry Wood and David Lloyd added 151 for the first wicket, Wood going on to 105. Clive Lloyd and Engineer then weighed in to take the score to 381 before Shuttleworth ripped through the Yorkshire top order, edging ever closer to the England call he was about to receive. There were four lower-order wickets for Lever before Yorkshire, 121 all out, were asked to follow on. A pulled muscle in his side now prevented Shuttleworth from taking the field, but the other bowlers rose to the challenge as the Yorkshire batsmen found the mountain too steep to climb. Victory by ten wickets was Lancashire's first in a Roses match for ten years. It took the county to the top of the table with 66 points, six ahead of Surrey, who had played two more matches.

'It was a great win that,' Jack says with relish, 'to beat them at Leeds, both teams pretty well at full strength. And, once we were winning games, confidence grew. It was just a case of switching them on really and leading them out. Everybody seemed to know what was expected of them without it being drummed down their throat all the time. In other words, they'd all grown up as cricketers by then.'

The next match almost brought Jack his revenge against Kent at Old Trafford, but the visitors, challenged to make 234 in two and a half hours, lost their ninth wicket to the final ball of the match while still 31 short of their target. In a summer when Old Trafford's excellent batting pitches made positive results hard to come by, the Gloucestershire match produced three declarations, but Jack's carrot – 256 in two hours and a half – could not entice the visiting batsmen. Against Warwickshire there were twin hundreds for Pilling, the second assisted by friendly bowling in its latter stages in a vain effort to entice a declaration, but the destructive power of John Jameson in the first innings made Jack reluctant to offer more than a token challenge.

Next, at Ilford, it was Lancashire's turn to chase a target, but the prospect of making 272 in three and a half hours on a pitch offering the bowlers some assistance ended with the batsmen grateful for a rain break as they staved off defeat with only one wicket intact. After the frustration of four draws in a row the challenge for the Championship was re-ignited when Middlesex came to Old Trafford. For this match Jack lost his two overseas players, who had both been recruited for the Rest of the World team whose five-match 'Test' series had been hastily set up once it was clear that a South African side could not be welcomed to the British Isles. Opposing them and winning a first England cap (as it was regarded at the time) was Ken Shuttleworth.

At 57 for five in reply to Middlesex's 344 for nine, Lancashire were deep in trouble. The follow on was in prospect, but two of the reserves rode to the rescue. Ken Snellgrove, with 138, and Frank Hayes, whose 94 came on his first-class debut, added 191, enabling Jack to close the Lancashire innings as soon as the Middlesex total had been passed. A second-innings declaration gave Lancashire two and three quarter hours in which to make 240. This was a generous challenge, to which Pilling responded by extending his run of good form with another century. Jack was with him as the last 34 runs were added to secure a five-wicket victory. 'I was very good at getting not outs when I was captain,' he quips, reminded that he had still been at the wicket with a useful 47 at the first innings declaration.

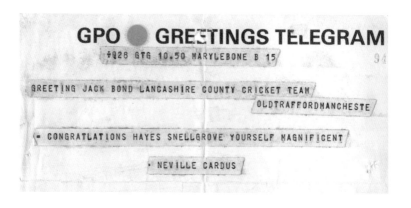

GPO ● GREETINGS TELEGRAM

⊤928 GTG 10.50 MARYLEBONE B 15

GREETING JACK BOND LANCASHIRE COUNTY CRICKET TEAM
OLDTRAFFORDMANCHESTE

= CONGRATLATIONS HAYES SNELLGROVE YOURSELF MAGNIFICENT

• NEVILLE CARDUS

Recognition from Sir Neville Cardus, of Lancashire's Championship win, over Middlesex, chasing runs at Old Trafford in June 1970.

With a match in hand over the championship leaders Surrey, Lancashire were now just four points behind. Perhaps the absent Clive Lloyd had played a part in securing the latest win – simply by not being there. Jack believes that the power of his hitting infused his colleagues with greater self-belief, but he ruefully reflects that Lancashire sometimes paid a price for Lloyd's genius: 'The targets that people left us gradually got more severe. They made their declarations against us with Clive in mind. And as Clive became better and better it made it harder for us.' The problem would intensify as the bid for the Championship strengthened. 'One of the problems is that the better you get at chasing and the higher you are in the Championship, the harder they set the targets for you, knowing that you're committed to giving it a go. Then you can get in trouble and end up looking for a draw.'

This was Lancashire's fate in their next engagement, against Hampshire at Southampton, where the home team dictated the shape of the match before Roy Marshall challenged Lancashire to make 259 at 78 an hour. When the last 20 overs began with just 99 needed and five wickets intact, victory had been in Lancashire's sights. Frank Hayes, in only his second match for the county, had set the innings alight, but when he fell one short of a maiden century, Lancashire's chances went with him. As in the Essex match, the county's lifeline was a last-wicket stand, this time between two stand-ins, keeper Keith Goodwin and pace bowler Mike Staziker, who survived eleven balls together to stave off defeat.

Manchester rain spoiled the Notts game, but the next match, against Somerset at Southport, brought a tantalising spectre of victory as Lancashire chased 162 in just under two hours. 'There was a kind of voluble hush around the ground, as near as Lancashire can get to the breathless variety,' wrote Alan Gibson in *The Times* as Shuttleworth faced up to the final over. With last man Lever for company and 12 runs required, he could manage only a pair of twos.

This was the third time in 12 championship matches that Lancashire had been taken to the brink of defeat with all resting on their last pair. Yet Jack's side were still undefeated in the Championship – a claim no other county could make – and, with a game in hand over the leaders, they remained well placed in the table:

	Played	Won	Lost	Drawn	Points
Surrey	13	5	1	7	133
Glamorgan	15	5	6	4	130
Sussex	15	4	3	8	129
Lancashire	12	4	0	8	126
Northants	14	4	3	7	126

Meanwhile, with nine matches played, Lancashire were clear leaders in the John Player table, their solitary loss the controversial rain-affected game against Kent, who now claimed second place, four points behind. The one-day specialists, as the team were dubbed, had also made good progress in the Gillette Cup. There had been a 27-run win against Gloucestershire at the end of May, and in early July Hampshire were beaten by five wickets at Old Trafford. With a place booked in the semi-final, there was heady talk of achieving cricket's new treble.

Jack now took his side to Lord's to complete a championship double against Middlesex, ten wickets for Lever and 99 by Wood leading the way to a ten-wicket win and another 17 points. With Surrey having no match, Sussex losing to Worcestershire and Glamorgan garnering only seven points from a drawn game with Essex, Lancashire were back on top of the table.

The next match was at Derby, where the home side, sixteenth in the Championship in 1969, had been enjoying a summer of better fortune. Winning the toss, Lancashire were in trouble when Jack came in at 127 for five. Now batting lower down the order at number seven, he had seldom been required to play a long innings and had hit just two half-centuries all summer, but his back-to-the-wall determination brought an invaluable 89 that only ended when, with the score at 270, he was run out. Declining to have the last man come to the wicket, Jack then declared to allow his bowlers a burst at the Derbyshire openers. It was the last time Lancashire would hold the initiative, the home side batting on into the third morning to post 468 for five against an attack shorn of Shuttleworth. In Lancashire's second knock, Jack was again top scorer with 58, but he was powerless to avoid the county sinking to a first championship defeat by ten wickets.

With a single bonus point earned from this match, the championship challenge had stuttered, but there was little time to brood with a Gillette semi-final the next day at Taunton. Before a capacity crowd, Lancashire lost the toss and had to field. The return of Clive Lloyd and Shuttleworth helped keep the Somerset batsmen in check, a total of 207 always being within Lancashire's compass in 60 overs. At 130 for five with Lloyd's enterprising innings over and Hayes immediately dismissed for a duck, Somerset could scent the possibility of victory, but Jack, with an undefeated 35, added 74 with Sullivan to snuff out their hopes, the winning hit coming with more than three overs to spare.

The treble was still in prospect, and a last-ball misfield in the other Gillette semi-final at The Oval meant that Sussex rather than Surrey would be contesting the final. Lancashire, the pedigree performers in one-day cricket, would be pitted against the side that had been the first to learn how to adjust to the challenge of the limited-overs game. But before the two teams could lock horns at Lord's there were nine championship matches to be played and no time for rest on Sundays as the three-pronged challenge moved closer to its climax.

With rain affecting the results of most of the next Sunday's John Player League matches, Lancashire were again among the victims of the competition rules after Surrey had won an important toss and chosen to field. Lancashire's 162 for six owed much to a stand of 51 between Jack and Hayes in the last nine of their 34 overs. But, coming at the end of the innings, their runs became academic once further rain had restricted the Surrey innings to 25 overs. Eventually requiring 106, the home batsmen reached their reduced target with two balls and two wickets to spare.

Lancashire remained top of the Sunday league table, but they now led by only four points from Derbyshire and Kent. Meanwhile rain continued to play its part in the Championship. There were only four points from a draw with Glamorgan at Blackpool, the match coming to a premature end with Lancashire in the ascendancy. Seven points were earned from an exciting draw at Hove where Sussex, with eight wickets down, ended only 16 short of their target. Back at Old Trafford, Manchester weather remained true to its reputation with only 20 minutes' play after the first day of the return match with Derbyshire, allowing Lancashire time to gather just two bowling points.

With other counties also suffering from the weather, Lancashire remained handily placed with a game or more in hand of most other contenders in a title race where the leaders were unusually tightly bunched:

	Played	Won	Lost	Drawn	Points
Surrey	18	5	1	12	166
Derbyshire	18	6	4	8	159
Sussex	20	4	5	11	158
Lancashire	17	5	1	11	157
Warwickshire	19	5	4	10	157
Glamorgan	18	6	6	6	155
Yorkshire	16	6	4	6	153

There was no game for Lancashire in the next round of championship matches – they had a three-day match against

Jamaica, which Jack missed, handing over the captaincy to David Lloyd. With Derbyshire and Yorkshire winning and others picking up bonus points, Jack's side slipped down to sixth place. Perhaps it was the Blackpool air that revived the team as they recorded their most emphatic win of the season. The Sussex total of 193 was soon made to look modest as David Lloyd and Wood posted 265, Lancashire's biggest opening partnership since Washbrook and Place had taken 233 and 350 off the same opponents in 1947. Capitulating for just 100 in their second innings, Sussex presented Lancashire with a victory in which *The Times* suggested that they had 'outplayed their opponents to a degree that must have been mildly embarrassing.'

This was to be the high point of Lancashire's championship season. Their next match was at Edgbaston but, after Saturday's play, the two teams, as if sponsored by a petrol company, travelled north to Old Trafford for their Sunday game. It was a wasted journey with rain allowing play for only 21 balls. Meanwhile Kent had a comfortable win against Gloucestershire at Cheltenham to reduce Lancashire's lead to a single point. 'A dramatic climax' to the Sunday league now seemed a possibility to *The Times*.

Back at Edgbaston for the championship match, Jack was last man out for 76, having shared an eighth-wicket partnership of 106 with Simmons to give Lancashire a useful lead of 121 on first innings. M.J.K.Smith, captaining Warwickshire in the absence of his namesake, then joined forces with Jameson in a stand of 230, delaying his declaration until Lancashire were required to make 179 in 25 minutes plus the final 20 overs. Knowing they had to go for the runs, Lancashire's batsmen sacrificed their wickets, Snellgrove and Pilling both being run out when set. With five overs to go and 54 still needed, Smith then brought on his 17-year-old leg-spinner Warwick Tidy to persuade Lancashire that victory might still be possible.

Tidy's two overs cost 16, but Smith's gamble had kept the game open. Simmons, his eye still on a win, holed out on the boundary off Lance Gibbs. It was only when their eighth wicket went down that Lancashire belatedly battened down the hatch. Fielders now crowded the bat as Gibbs began the final over. Off his first ball he induced a catch from Hughes, and from his sixth delivery he saw his captain snap up a catch in the gulley to dismiss Shuttleworth. This defeat, by 31 runs, was Jack's second in the Championship, but he could still reflect that no other county had lost so few.

Fourth in the table, Lancashire trailed Glamorgan by nine points. There were games in hand but, with five fixtures remaining, the last three matches would all be against fellow title challengers: Yorkshire, Glamorgan and Surrey.

Lancashire now faced the prospect of ten consecutive days of cricket, starting with a trip to New Road, where Worcestershire had yet to lose a championship match. Most of Saturday's play was lost to the weather, but the rain relented after the weekend to give the spinners a drying pitch. Jack declared Lancashire's first innings at 143 for six, still 25 adrift of the home side's total. His gesture was reciprocated by Norman Gifford, but none of Lancashire's challengers could have complained that Worcestershire's Ulverston-born skipper was showing his native county any special favours when he set a target of 220 in two hours and a half on a pitch tailor-made for his own bowling and that of fellow left-armer Doug Slade. Lancashire soon slumped to 74 for seven, only 18 overs of stern defence from Hayes and Hughes staving off defeat.

The Red Rose frustrations in the Championship, which continued in a high-scoring draw at Trent Bridge later in the week, had again been set aside for the Sabbath. Beating Worcestershire by 39 runs meant that only Kent, five points adrift but with a game in hand, could prevent Lancashire retaining their John Player title.

Victory at Old Trafford on the Sunday would seal the first leg of the treble. Meanwhile, with only ten points separating the top six teams, no side was better placed than Lancashire in the Championship:

	Played	Won	Lost	Drawn	Points
Glamorgan	22	8	6	8	200
Derbyshire	23	7	6	10	195
Lancashire	21	6	2	13	195
Yorkshire	22	7	5	10	193
Surrey	21	6	3	12	192
Kent	21	7	5	9	190

The script writer's dream was coming true, the schedule bringing to Old Trafford the traditional Bank Holiday opponents, Yorkshire. The two counties were due to start a championship match on the Saturday before breaking off for the one-day decider on the Sunday. For good measure Jack had chosen the championship game for his benefit.

The overture was promising. On the Saturday, Lancashire, 346 for four, were moving towards their highest championship total of the season. The next day is one that Jack will never forget. *The Guardian,* with commendable precision, reported a gate of 27,559, 'many of whom had never been to a cricket match before.' Reporting some nine months later, *Wisden* was more inclined to guess: 'For the first time since 1948 the gates were closed with a crowd of nearly 33,000 watching,' its match report states, though the Almanack elsewhere admits that 'the official figures gave the crowd as 27,000 but several more thousand stormed into Old Trafford by devious means just before the gates were closed.' Devious means! Jack's own recollection is of more straightforward action. 'They stormed the gates to get in. They knocked the main gate down, the big wooden car park gate, they flattened it. Then, of course, they got into the ground. They estimated there were about 6,000 on the grass.'

There was a cloudless sky as Jack won the toss and decided to field. Yorkshire's rock was Geoff Boycott, but for lack of support he could hardly blame team-mates. Fellow opener Doug Padgett was run out after Boycott refused his call and, later in the innings, John Woodford sacrificed his wicket to save the great man. There were some promising strokes from Sharpe and Close, but at 142 for five, three wickets fell in the same over from Shuttleworth, the first of them Boycott to a tumbling catch by Jack, described by Eric Todd in the *Manchester Guardian* as 'magnificent'. There were some bitten nails as Lancashire, in need of 166, lost Engineer early then found the overs ticking by before Clive Lloyd gave the innings momentum, but after he was out at 93, it was two of Jack's sometimes unsung heroes, Pilling and Sullivan, who finished the business, each passing 50.

Writing in *The Times,* John Woodcock captured the emotions of the day in remembering those who had staunchly supported Lancashire through the empty years. Now they were hearing 'the sounds that ordinarily only come from the football in the distance.' Beside his report was a picture of Jack's crucial catch, its caption carrying the message that it epitomised 'the sort of fielding that has helped his team retain the John Player League title.'

Sobriety returned to Old Trafford as the championship game resumed on the Monday in front of a crowd of 10,000. Jack allowed his batsmen to pile on the runs, declaring at 430 for seven. Wood, with 144, scored his second Roses hundred of the season, while Pilling, Clive Lloyd and Hayes all posted half-centuries. Jack meanwhile maintained his reputation for saving his runs for when they were most needed, contributing just a single – the run traditionally allowed to all beneficiaries.

Jack's tactics ensured that the championship pennant would not be flying over Headingley, but meant that his only realistic route to victory was to enforce the follow on and bowl Yorkshire out twice. However, with Boycott dropping anchor for 98, only three Yorkshire wickets had fallen by the close of play, one of the victims the hapless Padgett who found Boycott unresponsive to his call for the second time in 24 hours. Yorkshire declared their first innings 148 behind in the hope of squeezing an enticing gesture from Jack, but some pedestrian batting was the prelude to a closure that challenged Yorkshire to make 210 in 50 minutes plus the final 20 overs. Even before Boycott was out to the first ball of the innings, it was never a serious prospect.

John Woodcock, anticipating some of the excitement of Sunday's match, had stayed on at Old Trafford, but he now felt compelled to describe the conclusion of the match as 'the poorest day's play I have seen all season.' He told his *Times* readers that 'neither Close nor Bond was prepared to make a genuine bid for victory and that, in Lancashire's case, must have maddened their supporters.' Challenged to answer this denigration of his captaincy, Jack says, 'It's our Test match, the Roses Match.' There is little need for elaboration: to avoid losing to Yorkshire is, for Lancashire supporters, a priority that transcends all others.

The stalemate at Old Trafford was good news for Glamorgan, who had strengthened hopes of retaining their title with a nervy four-wicket win against Derbyshire at Swansea. With some counties having completed their championship programme, several contenders were still tightly bunched behind the leaders, but it was Kent, bottom of the table at the beginning of July, who were now emerging as the pace setters. Beating Nottinghamshire at Folkestone with just three wickets and eight balls in hand, they had now won four of their last five matches.

	Played	Won	Lost	Drawn	Points
Glamorgan	23	9	6	8	218
Kent	22	8	5	9	206
Lancashire	22	6	2	14	200
Derbyshire	24	7	7	10	199
Sussex	24	5	7	12	199
Warwickshire	23	7	6	10	198
Surrey	22	6	4	12	196
Yorkshire	23	7	5	11	196

Lancashire, Kent and Surrey all had a game in hand on Glamorgan, whose programme was about to be completed with a visit from Lancashire, whose players were hastening from Old Trafford to catch their train for the showdown at Cardiff once stumps had been drawn in the Roses match.

Though both sides were eager to start, heavy overnight rain and squally showers into the afternoon kept the players in the pavilion, and only 90 minutes' play was possible on the first day. Resuming at 59 for no wicket and needing to make up lost time, Lancashire batted with great enterprise the following day, rattling up 243 for three by lunch. It was Clive Lloyd who set the initial pace with a run-a-minute 59, Pilling and Sullivan weighing in later. With six batting points in the bank, Jack declared on 303 for five at the end of the 85th over. His bowlers then set to work. By close of play they had kept the dream of the grand slam alive by reducing Glamorgan to 138 for seven, still in need of 16 runs to avoid the follow on.

Next day there was the perfect start. Shuttleworth took the last three wickets in five balls and, after Jack had enforced the follow-on, Glamorgan were soon in deeper trouble. At 50 for two they had lost both their overseas players, Bryan Davis and Majid Khan, and Geoff Ellis had been forced to retire after being hit on the head. As Lancashire began to scent victory, Peter Walker joined forces with his captain Tony Lewis. Watchful at first, the pair moved quickly through the gears after lunch, Walker at one point scoring 67 off his own bat in 25 minutes and going on to 114 as the partnership reached 195.

Jack seemed powerless to stem the flow, causing John Woodcock to wonder if he was saving his bowlers for the next day's Lord's final. Or, with the pennant flying at Sophia Gardens for perhaps the last time, had Jack foreseen the Quixotic and desperate gesture Lewis was about to make to keep it in Wales for one more year?

When the declaration came, Lancashire had 15 overs in which to make 137. What might be seen as a challenging target in the age of Twenty20 was an improbable mission in 1970, while the defending champions, in John Woodcock's view, had no more than a thousand-to-one chance of success. Conceding that Lewis's remote prospect of glory could justify his gesture, Woodcock still opined that 'by bringing Lancashire back into the game, Glamorgan might have persuaded the people of Kent to march in their fury upon them.'

Needing to score at just over nine runs an over, Jack sent in Clive Lloyd and Engineer, while he and Sullivan padded up in readiness to have a go. Eleven runs came from the first over, but the last ball of the second saw Lloyd beaten by Bryan Davis' fine throw from the long-on boundary as he attempted a second run. With Engineer also perishing early, the target was beyond the remaining batsmen. Two overs remained to be bowled when the match ended in anti-climax with Lancashire on 77 for five. Their consolation was 11 bonus points to Glamorgan's two, but an innings defeat of Leicestershire brought 23 points to Kent, which took them past Glamorgan in the table and virtually ended Lancashire's hopes.

There were mixed emotions as the players scrambled onto their train to Paddington, their sights now fixed on the Gillette final. Unthinkably to the more cosseted players of the modern game, when they booked into their Clarendon Court hotel at eleven o'clock that night, they were within twelve hours of taking the field at nearby Lord's. Meanwhile, back in Lancashire, many of the team's wives, not permitted to join their husbands at the hotel, would have been gathering at the Bond home, where Florence would accommodate as many as she could before they all set off at the crack of dawn to join the excitement.

Five of the Sussex team were survivors of the side that had won the first two limited-overs finals in 1963 and 1964, and they had as rich a one-day tradition as any county, but for the Lancashire players memories of performing in front of a capacity crowd were just six days old, and their supporters were in full voice in the glorious Lord's sunshine as Jack won the toss.

Deciding to field allowed his players to parade their strongest suit. Clive Lloyd, their inspiration, soon made his mark on the match. Hesitant running in the early stages and three run outs towards the end of the innings complemented tight bowling to keep the

Sussex innings in check. David Hughes, with the wickets of Jim Parks, Tony Greig and Peter Graves, all bowled, at a cost of 31, was the most successful of the bowlers as Sussex were contained to 184 for nine in their 60 overs.

It should have been easy for Lancashire, but at 37 for two David Lloyd and Barry Wood were out. The stage was now set for Clive Lloyd. With some memorable strokes he took the score to 86, but his 29 runs were a cameo when an innings of substance was required. 'I think he felt at the time he got out that our best chance of winning had gone,' Jack remembers. But the diminutive Harry Pilling, with whom Lloyd would share many partnerships in the cause of the Red Rose, buckled down, taking Lancashire past the winning post and earning the Man of the Match award for his undefeated 70.

Jack is fulsome in his praise of Pilling, 'such a proud Lancastrian', and feels that his innings had a wider significance for the county's cricket: 'Harry played a tremendous innings and guided us home. I think that did Clive quite a lot of good, and it did us all a lot of good when we suddenly realised that it was all down to teamwork and, even if your best player fails, the rest of you pull together to put it right again. It took a bit of pressure off Clive as well. I think he played his cricket for Lancashire from then on in the more relaxed atmosphere that we'd created, even though he was the great Clive Lloyd.'

The six-wicket victory over Sussex was to be the height of Lancashire's dreams. The next week Kent took eight points from a rain-ruined championship match against Surrey, so when Lancashire returned to London the following Saturday, only a cricketing miracle in their match with Surrey could bring them the title. A record 27 points – only possible if their batsmen could score 450 in 85 overs – were needed for Lancashire to be crowned champions. The bowlers did their stuff, claiming all ten Surrey wickets to secure the five points that would ensure third place, but so much rain had fallen that the match was in its final day before the last Surrey wicket fell. Lancashire then closed their season in sadly feeble style, sliding to 58 for seven.

Two one-day titles had been convincingly won, but domestic cricket's greatest prize remained elusive. That autumn, Jack was chosen by the Professional Cricketers' Association as their Player of the Year, and the following spring there was one further

*Jack and Farokh Engineer hold the Gillette Cup aloft
at Lord's, 5 September 1970.*

*The Lancashire side
which won the John Player League and the Gillette Cup in 1970.
Standing (l to r): B.Wood, J.Simmons, D.Lloyd, D.P.Hughes, J.Sullivan,
F.C.Hayes, K.Shuttleworth.
Seated: P.Lever, H.Pilling, J.D.Bond (capt), F.M.Engineer (wk), C.H.Lloyd.*

accolade when he was named as one of *Wisden's* five Cricketers of the Year. John Kay in his essay extolling the virtues of the man from Little Hulton concluded by saying of Jack that he 'may not be cricket's most talented captain, but he is certainly the game's most enthusiastic leader. No man with anything less to offer could have revitalised Lancashire cricket, so comprehensively, so soon.'

Lionel Lister presents Jack with a salver at a celebration dinner at the Anglo-American Sporting Club after Lancashire had won the Gillette and John Player League competitions. Neil Durden-Smith looks on.

Chapter Ten

'A great catch to end a great innings'

Two one-day trophies had Lancashire's name engraved upon them, but as a new season dawned, the perennial challenge still faced the captain. Could 1971 bring an end to the long drought and see the Championship return to Old Trafford for the first time since 1934? 'That was the main one at the start of every season I can remember,' says Jack. 'Even when the other competitions came along, even then, the thing that the old Lancastrians, the committee and the rest were desperate to win was the County Championship.' Just a few years earlier Lancashire had been perpetual no-hopers, but a London bookmaker now installed the county as favourite for each of the three competitions, although at 5 to 1 against Jack's team were rated less favourably for the Championship than for the Gillette, where they were quoted at 4 to 1, and the John Player League, where the price was down to 5 to 2.

Jack certainly had a powerful squad at his command. It was a timely reflection on the progress of the younger players he had helped to nurture, that four – Hayes, Hughes, Pilling and Shuttleworth – should be chosen to represent MCC in the seasonal opener against the champion county at Lord's. In the campaign that lay ahead for Jack there was unlikely to be a shortage of Red Rose runs. The attack was led by two England pace bowlers, albeit that Lever and Shuttleworth had both had a tiring winter in Australia and New Zealand, but Jack could also call on a pair of spinners, Hughes and Simmons, now growing in experience, who gave him a balanced attack in a season when a new regulation required pitches to be left uncovered once a match had started.

Beating Gloucestershire by an innings at Bristol got the championship season under way in the best possible fashion, but this early form was not maintained. There was a second win in late May, when Hughes and Simmons bowled out a Glamorgan side still chasing victory at Swansea 'when all rational hope was gone', but Lancashire did not taste success again until the last match in June, when a six-wicket victory at Northampton came, after three declarations, from the first ball of the final over. These three wins had been partly offset by two defeats, but a decent haul of bonus points had helped to keep the leaders within sight.

Against Nottinghamshire, at Old Trafford, a Garry Sobers declaration allowed Clive Lloyd to lead the way to another six-wicket success. An eight-wicket loss to Kent at Southport was a setback, but then Lancashire returned to the winning trail, completing the double over Northants at Old Trafford. Jack had been having a quiet time with the bat, but he now took the chance to score his only fifty of the summer as he and Hughes set up a target for the visitors to chase. Northants' goal was 302, but once Lever and Shuttleworth had reduced them to 5 for six, victory became a formality. Lancashire were now back in the championship race. On 17 July they shared the lead with Warwickshire, though with two more matches played.

	Played	Won	Lost	Drawn	Points
Warwickshire	13	5	4	4	144
Lancashire	15	5	3	7	144
Middlesex	14	5	2	7	138
Surrey	14	6	1	7	133
Kent	13	5	2	6	133

While the championship challenge had taken time to gather momentum, the John Player League had also been asking more questions of Lancashire. There were three defeats in the first six matches before the tide turned, the only loss in the next eight games coming in the tightest of finishes when Lancashire ended on 199 for seven in pursuit of 202 against Nottinghamshire at Trent Bridge. Needing to hit the final ball for six to win the match, Hughes managed only three, while Jack, on one of the few Sundays when he was required to play an innings of any substance, ended undefeated on 24.

The winning habit was once again filling the grounds wherever Lancashire went. At Headingley, in front of Yorkshire's biggest home crowd, Clive Lloyd, with 97 not out, led Lancashire to 239 for four and victory by 48 runs. This win brought a share of third place with Leicestershire, four points behind Worcestershire and five adrift of Somerset. With the challenge ignited in the Championship and Sunday league, the Lancashire team were fighting on three fronts, their place in the semi-final of the Gillette Cup already assured.

Sir Neville Cardus (left) with John Savage, Jack and Bert Flack, groundsman at Old Trafford, 1971.

Gillette success had started with comfortable wins over Somerset at Taunton and Worcestershire at New Road, but the Somerset game brought Jack an unusual scare. The match had started on a Saturday, but 42 overs into the Somerset innings, rain had forced play to be abandoned until the Monday. While the Somerset team had to travel for their Sunday league match to Ilkeston, Lancashire languished in their hotel with no game. That evening Jack set a 10.30 curfew and he was sitting in the hotel when a policeman arrived with a grave expression, looking for a Mr Jack Bond, captain of Lancashire. 'I said, "I'm Jack Bond. What's the problem?" He said, "I've got two of your players outside." I knew who it was going to be – Harry Pilling and John Sullivan. I thought, what have they been up to now? He said, "We've caught them urinating down a side street. We're going to have to lock them up and put them in front of the magistrates in the morning." I said, "You can't do that. We're halfway through a Gillette Cup match." He said, "Well I'm sorry, but that's what's got to happen." The policeman set off for the door, and the next thing John and Harry came running in. They'd put the copper up to it. It had frightened the life out of me!'

The third-round match, against Essex at Chelmsford, was a closer run affair. There could hardly have been a worse start for Lancashire after Jack had chosen to bat and then seen Wood, David Lloyd and Pilling all dismissed for just 16. Clive Lloyd, already Man of the Match for his 83 not out against Worcestershire, was again the pillar without which the Lancashire innings would have foundered. He had been involved, if not wholly culpable, in the run out of his namesake, and the only way he could repay his colleagues was to make runs. Partners came and went, Jack among them, until Simmons stayed to add 91 while Lloyd went on to 109 out of his team's 203 for seven.

The Essex innings also started badly, but a spirited knock by Keith Boyce was followed by a seventh-wicket stand of 74 between Stuart Turner and Robin Hobbs. Only 18 were needed from 19 balls, when Lever and Shuttleworth induced injudicious shots to straight balls, Hobbs, in the words of John Woodcock, 'going for a glance that would have tested Ranji at his best.' With the quicker men bowled out, the final over was entrusted to Hughes. He needed just two balls to settle frayed nerves and edge his side home by 12 runs.

Clive Lloyd took another Man of the Match award, but the memory Jack carries of his innings is of a call for gloves halfway through his innings. 'He didn't need to change his gloves, but he had to get a message to the twelfth man. Clive had just seen his fiancée in one of the stands trying to get into a seat. He'd forgotten to get her sorted out with a complimentary ticket. He's in the middle of this crucial innings in a Gillette tie and he spots Waveney all that way off!'

The semi-final brought Lancashire their first home game in the competition – and a match that would be etched in the annals of one-day cricket. Jack remembers the excitement the tie generated as both counties' supporters converged on the ground: 'The roads were chock-a-block. The lads were told to get in early because we'd experienced big crowds before.' Winning the toss and opting to chase a target, Jack led his men out as a capacity crowd thronged the stands in eager anticipation.

Athletic fielding kept the score in check and lunch was taken at 83 for one after 33 overs. Spectators, who had basked in warm sunshine at the start, now learned that it is always a wise precaution to take an umbrella to Old Trafford. An hour was lost to rain. When play resumed, Gloucestershire's second wicket soon fell, bringing their danger man Mike Procter to the crease. Starting with circumspection, he was soon expanding his strokes and beating the field on both sides of the wicket. Procter's 65 made sure his side would post a challenging total but, needing 230 for victory, Jack still felt confident of winning: 'I never thought that they'd got enough runs, though it was one of the bigger totals at the time,' he says. He was not to know the impact the lost hour would have on the game.

There was 50 from Wood and, with the other early batsmen all making useful contributions, Lancashire were well placed at 160 for four. Off-spinner John Mortimore then bowled Clive Lloyd and he claimed a second wicket three runs later when Engineer hit his stumps in completing his shot. At 163 for six, with two new batsmen at the crease and the light starting to deteriorate, it was a different story.

At 7.30 the umpires could have called the game off for the day, but their instructions encouraged them to complete it if at all possible, so play continued. Jack was at the wicket with Simmons as the light got steadily worse. He had not bargained for this when he had won the toss and he could still have come off. But although he now feared that Lancashire would be beaten, he preferred to give the crowd its money's worth. 'With the ground jam-packed full, it would have been such an anticlimax to continue the match the following day.'

In light that *Wisden* described as 'murky to the say the least' Simmons was striking the ball well. 'It was getting darker and darker,' Jack recalls. 'And they were taking longer and longer to bowl their overs. But they were also getting very tired because they'd had to field for close to 50 overs without a break.' The two Jacks had added 40 in seven overs when Mortimore struck again, bowling Simmons.

Twenty-seven were needed from the last six overs when David Hughes came in. Only Lever and Shuttleworth were to follow. 'We were obviously going to finish now,' says Jack. 'We'd have got lynched if we'd gone off then with four or five overs still to go. We had to carry on. Our hands were tied; we'd got no choice. It looked as though we were going to get beaten, but we also knew that they were having difficulty seeing the ball.'

Hughes came down the wicket to meet Jack. 'Do you think we can win?' he asked his skipper. 'I said, "You've got to give it a go. You can hit it." He said, "If I can see it, I'll hit it."' Mortimore, an accomplished Test bowler, had taken Gloucestershire to the brink of victory. But now, Jack reckons, his opponents made the wrong decision. 'They played into our hands because they kept with

Mortimore when they could have bowled one of their seamers. It gave us a chance to put bat to ball – and that's just what David did. I said, 'If you're going to hit it, hit through it, don't drag across it. Hit it straight if you can.'"

With fielders struggling to sight the ball, there were two sixes, two fours and two twos as 24 were taken from the over. Taking heed of his captain's advice, Hughes had dragged only one of the shots towards mid-wicket. The scores were now level. As the hands of the clock passed ten to nine, Jack nudged the fifth ball of Procter's next over off his hips for a single to take Lancashire to another Lord's final. He had made only 16 of the 67 runs added since he came to the wicket, but he had kept his head and his wise counsel had helped the young David Hughes take the Man of the Match award.

David Hughes remembers that they 'had decided to get them all off Morty, as we wouldn't have been able to pick the quickies up. Jack Simmons had shouted from the balcony after I had hit three balls of the over to calm down and look for singles. I'm glad I didn't hear him. The champagne flowed and I took a glass to John Mortimore – as a player, I knew just how he must have felt.'

Jack looks back on one of cricket's most amazing finishes: 'Goodness knows what would have happened if we'd only got two or three in that over and we'd been into another over and another! It was the longest day of my life. It was after midnight before we could get away from the ground with all the celebrations.'

The twilight drama behind them, Lancashire still had other business on the agenda. There had been stumbles in the Championship. At Derby, Jack had reinforced his reputation as a good man for a crisis with a patient 41 as he and Engineer added 168, thus gaining six batting points from an innings that had once been tottering at 33 for four. There was a brief but unavailing tilt at victory in the second innings before survival became the priority. The exhilaration of the twilight match in the Gillette was then sandwiched by an uninspiring draw with Somerset on a docile Old Trafford pitch, and a Roses match at Sheffield ended by rain when already heading for a draw.

Hopes of a championship challenge revived at Edgbaston where, for the second year, Warwickshire captain Mike Smith timed his declaration to set up an exciting challenge with victory again coming off the very last ball – this time to Lancashire. The final over had started with ten runs still needed. Jack was at the wicket with Shuttleworth. When his partner hit the third ball for six to level the scores, Jack tried in vain for the winning run and perished, leaving it to Keith Goodwin to scramble a leg bye off the last ball.

This win lifted Lancashire back to second place in the table, eight points behind the team they had just beaten, but with one more match played. Meanwhile Surrey hovered ominously, a further 29 points behind but with three matches in hand. The treble was still on the cards, but rain allowed Lancashire only three points from the Middlesex match at Blackpool and a 75-run defeat at Leicester in another watery game left Lancashire 18 points behind the leaders, their sights now on the one-day titles.

There had been a happier outcome when Lancashire had visited Grace Road earlier in the month for their John Player match. Once again Hughes was the hero of the hour. Coming in with eight needed from the last five balls, he struck a four and a six to extend Lancashire's winning sequence and claim top spot in the table for the first time. The quirks of the fixture list meant that Lancashire now had two blank Sundays, but challengers with games in hand let their chances slip. When the matches on 22 August had all been played, the prospect of a Red Rose hat trick of John Player titles had moved from hope towards expectation:

	Played	Won	Tied	Lost	N/R	Points
Lancashire	14	10	0	4	0	40
Essex	15	10	0	5	0	40
Somerset	16	9	0	5	2	38
Worcestershire	14	9	0	5	0	36
Leicestershire	15	9	0	6	0	36

With a game in hand over Essex and a superior run rate over other challengers, Lancashire could make sure of the title by beating Worcestershire at Old Trafford. Fate now stepped in, decreeing that Manchester should be targeted for a torrential downpour, but both teams were determined to play and at five o'clock a ten-over contest began. It was Lancashire's turn to skid around the field first, in 'near farcical' conditions, as Worcestershire, with 36 from Ron Headley, reached 77 for three. With no fielding restrictions or limit on the bowlers' overs – Lever and Shuttleworth operated throughout – this was a good score in an era where the switch hit and the paddle sweep were still to be invented. It proved too much for Lancashire, for whom only Sullivan and David Lloyd, in the traditional words of *Wisden*, 'showed the necessary soundness.' Losing wickets like gamblers on state benefit, they finished on 67 for seven. Defeat now meant a two-week wait for the season's final round of matches, when victory against Glamorgan would secure the title.

Meanwhile, there had been a belated upturn of fortunes in the Championship. At Bournemouth Jack's well-timed declaration, setting Hampshire 217 in two and a half hours, brought victory by 14 runs with ten balls remaining. The batsmen then chased down a target of 245 in two and three quarter hours to beat Derbyshire by four wickets at Old Trafford. The last championship game, played around the fateful John Player match at Old Trafford, brought an innings defeat of Worcestershire, whose batting folded first to Shuttleworth and then to the spinners, with Simmons taking three wickets in his final over to close the championship season in style.

With their programme of matches ending early, on 31 August, Lancashire miraculously led the Championship:

	Played	Won	Lost	Drawn	Points
Lancashire	24	9	4	11	241
Warwickshire	23	8	9	6	232
Surrey	21	10	2	9	226
Kent	23	7	6	10	226

For Lancashire the hope was that there might be enough rain for Noah to re-float his ark. It was not to be. In the end they had done enough to retain third place, their tally of points 25 higher than in 1970, while the champions, ultimately Surrey with Warwickshire equal on points, finished with just 14 more than Lancashire.

This year there was no scramble for the train on the eve of the Gillette Cup final. While there was an early evening journey from Trent Bridge for the Kent players, Lancashire enjoyed three days' respite. 'Knock out experts lack Kent's flexibility' *The Times* predicted, telling its readers that 'not even for the Saturday of a Lord's Test match is there a keener sense of anticipation than there will be around the ground this morning.'

In his hotel bed Jack had lain awake. 'I didn't sleep very well the night before. It's something that does get to you over the years as a captain – your mind is sort of ticking over. Such a vital game! We'd won in 1970 and then having had this semi-final, you think our luck is going to run out some time. Maybe it will be this game against Kent!' Jack is not a man given to suspicions, but he was receptive to them now. 'There was a Kent umpire – we didn't think that was a good omen.'

Arthur Fagg was on the Test panel at the time, but might he still have a leaning towards the county for whom he had played over 400 matches? The initial portents were not reassuring. The second ball of the match, from John Dye, cannoned into Wood's pads and Fagg's finger was raised. Back in the pavilion Jack remembers the opener's return. 'Barry came in and said he'd hit it and there was a big red mark on the edge of his bat. Then he gave one against Harry Pilling that everyone thought was a bit high. He's only five foot two anyway, but Harry thought it was high!' Sixty-six from Clive Lloyd was again the mainstay of the innings, but it took some muscular slogs from Simmons and Hughes, with 39 added in the last four overs, to lift Lancashire to 224 for seven.

Jack leads out his team at Lord's in the 1971 Gillette final, when Lancashire won by 24 runs.

England opener Brian Luckhurst fell immediately to Lever and, with four men out for 68, the initiative was with Lancashire. But Kent skipper Asif Iqbal remained cool, his classical strokes unfurling to dominate partnerships with Alan Knott, John

Shepherd and the young Bob Woolmer. The score rose steadily, and at 197 for six Kent were on course for a comfortable win. For Jack it was the last throw of the dice – he needed his best one-day bowler to stem the flow. 'It got to the stage where it was going so well for Kent that if I waited another over to bring Jack Simmons on to put it in the block-hole, it would have probably been too late. So, in desperation really, I brought him on at the Pavilion end.'

The Pavilion end, accentuating turn into the batsman, is conventionally favoured by off-spinners at Lord's, but Jack always saw it differently in limited overs games. 'I can defend straight balls, and at Lord's you always feel the boundaries are short and it runs away from you down the slope.' Jack Simmons remembers the challenge of bowling to a batsman as quick on his feet as Asif, who could turn his block-hole balls into full tosses: 'I thought I'll try something else. I'll try one on off stump, and because he was giving himself just that little bit of room he reached for it and wasn't quite at the pitch of the ball. But I still thought, crikey, that's another four through extra cover.' Seeing the ball destined for the corner of the Warner Stand, Lancashire supporters' hearts sank. But all was not lost. In the words of John Arlott, writing in the *Guardian*: 'Bond, shedding half his thirty-nine years, leapt up wide to his right and took the catch one-handed at full stretch before falling, holding it exultantly high.'

Lancashire's captain had taken a miracle catch that would be talked of for decades to come. For Arlott, 'all that came after was anti-climax.' To John Woodcock, too, it was the game's last turning point. 'He [Asif] had turned impending defeat into imminent victory when Bond had his moment of inspiration. It took a great catch to end a great innings, and by the way they mobbed their captain Lancashire showed their relief. A brilliant piece of fielding by Clive Lloyd, which ran out Julien, rounded off this happy day.'

Lancashire's luck had held. Only one more encounter remained to round off another successful season. The following Sunday, 30,000 were again crammed into Old Trafford. They had come to salute their champions and witness the coup de grâce in the John Player League. At first the script was followed faithfully. Glamorgan batted and brilliant fielding took the eye as only Majid Khan and Tony Lewis threatened an innings of any substance. 'We managed to restrict them to 143 and everybody thought it was won,' Jack reflects sadly. From 43 for one the innings disintegrated. There was a brief flurry of hitting from Hughes, but the match was lost by 34 runs and with it went £750 worth of prize money that the team might have shared out as champions.

Clive Lloyd's wedding had taken place the previous day. It took the blame for the shortcomings of the Lancashire batsmen, but Jack maintains that this was unfair: 'We left the wedding reasonably early. We were beaten by a better side on the day. But it would have been lovely to have won the John Player three times instead of twice.'

Chapter Eleven
'The finest captain I played under'

Jack was 40 when the 1972 season began. He had glimpsed the summit in the past two seasons, but the Championship had proved elusive. He still had the same players around him and to their number had now been added Peter Lee from Northants, as cover in case Lever and Shuttleworth should be called for Test duty. Seen at first as a questionable signing, Lee would go on to serve with distinction and be chosen, in 1976, as one of *Wisden's* Cricketers of the Year.

As the summer unfolded, Jack began to accept that it would probably be his last as a first-team player. 'I couldn't maintain the standard in the field that I'd expected of everybody when we first started,' he says. Perhaps, too, his captaincy was getting a bit stale: 'As a school coach you are saying the same things every year to a different group of boys, but now I was saying the same things as I was saying five years ago to the same group of people.'

It was soon clear that there would be no fairy-tale ending in the Championship, where only two matches were won against three losses, and Lancashire sank to fifteenth. In a wretchedly wet summer, when the North-West always suffers disproportionately, no side drew more matches, but as if to show the wisdom of signing Lee, both Lever and Shuttleworth bowled below par in a season when too few bowling points were earned. Jack's own batting seldom fired, though he gave one nostalgic glimpse of his best with an undefeated 103 against Middlesex at Lord's, his only three-figure score in his years as captain. It came on a pitch of 'variable bounce' from which Wood had earlier been taken to hospital, and was only made possible by a partnership of 78 for the last wicket with Lee, whose 18 was his highest score of the season.

The one-day competitions offered the side more hope. But there was a quarter-final exit from the new Benson and Hedges Cup and only eighth place was achieved in the Sunday League, where it was agreed in mid-season that Jack should stand down from the captaincy to help ease in David Lloyd, his planned successor. The one bright spot was the Gillette Cup, where the team survived a rough passage to reach Lord's and give Jack his chance to retire with a hat trick of wins.

Somerset were defeated by seven runs at Old Trafford, then consistent batting brought a four-wicket victory over Hampshire at Bournemouth, after a Barry Richards century had set a target of 224. There was another close finish at a damp Old Trafford, where Kent went down by seven runs. Lancashire's win came after Cowdrey and Denness had elected to play on in poor light on the first day. A crowd of 20,000 should not be disappointed, they had felt, a decision that cost them Cowdrey's wicket to the last ball before the players left the field. Next day, fortunes fluctuated as Simmons gave Lancashire the initiative with three wickets in 15 balls, only to be hit for 17 in an over by Bernard Julien. But, in the words of *The Times*, 'Bond by his field placings made twos as scarce as threes and fours,' and it was Simmons who had the final say. Twelve were needed when Hughes began the final over and it was the safe hands of his spinning partner on the boundary edge that pouched a lofted drive from John Shepherd off the first ball, leaving the last pair with too much to do.

So, for the third year in succession, Lancashire's army of fans descended on Lord's. Jack remembers this final for the mystery he managed to create over his team selection. Thirteen players and a twelfth man were taken down to London for the match against Warwickshire, but Jack was concerned about the fitness of Lever and Shuttleworth, who had both sustained injuries a month earlier. 'I didn't want to go into a final and have one or both quick bowlers breaking down with another ten overs to bowl or something like that. I didn't want to be worrying about that all the time.' The captains went out to toss, club captain Alan Smith undertaking the job for Warwickshire, although he was not himself playing in the match. It was at this point that Jack revealed his hand.

'I had the coin and I said, "We've got 13 players, but Lever and Shuttleworth aren't playing." And Alan Smith didn't know whether to look at the coin. I'd won the toss and I said, "You can bat." And they came in wondering who was going to open the bowling.' Jack's choice was Clive Lloyd, who bowled his twelve overs on the trot for just 31 runs, and Lee.

Peter Lever, who quotes Jack's tactics as a brilliant piece of captaincy, maintains that he and Shuttleworth were both perfectly fit and keen to play, but he knew that Jack's plan was to have bowlers who would get through their overs quickly. 'So they'd be playing for lunch, then playing themselves in again after lunch and there wouldn't be too many overs left.' Three run-outs in the latter stages were evidence of the plan's success, but the strong Warwickshire batting line-up nevertheless reached 234 for nine, setting a target that had never been achieved in a decade of finals. There was a sedate response for a while before Clive Lloyd opened his shoulders to play, in the words of *Wisden*, 'one of the finest innings imaginable', his 126 ensuring that the match was won by four wickets with more than three overs to spare.

Cedric Rhoades, Farokh Engineer, Jack Simmons and Jack Bond
with the trophy after the 1972 Gillette final.
Jack remains the only captain who has won the knock-out competition three times.

The season was rounded off when Kent, as winners of the John Player League, returned to Old Trafford to play a challenge match against Lancashire as Gillette winners. The home side won by just four runs. By this time, though, Jack had played his last innings for Lancashire – c Hemmings b Jameson 18 – dismissed shortly before Warwickshire were beaten by four wickets in the season's last John Player match.

Jack bids farewell to the Lancashire team in 1972.

The man who had been appointed 'until we find someone else' had led Lancashire for five years. Stephen Chalke, in an article for the *Wisden Cricketer*, has shown that only two county captains, Mark Alleyne with Gloucestershire and Mike Denness at Kent, have exceeded Jack's five one-day titles but, whereas Alleyne's seven successes came from 24 opportunities and Denness led Kent in 17 campaigns for his six victories, Jack's five titles were won after leading his side in just ten limited-over competitions.

For Farokh Engineer, who speaks in reverential tones of his first Bombay captain Polly Umrigar, and who went on to play his 46 Tests under five different men, Jack remains 'the finest captain I ever played under.' To Peter Lever, who developed into an England player under Jack, he was 'a fabulous captain. I was very fortunate in that Jack Bond and Raymond Illingworth, my England captain, were the two best captains in the country.'

What made a journeyman player such an outstandingly successful captain? Clive Lloyd has no doubts: 'Jack's great strength was that he knew about teamwork. He was such a good man personally that you wanted to do well for him.' 'He was such a lovable person,' says Farokh Engineer. 'Everybody wanted to play for Bondy. Nobody took advantage of him.' Being a Lancastrian to the core, and one who had come through the ranks, commended him to his players, but for Jack Simmons it was also the emphasis he put on team values, with no place for prima donnas, that was the essence of his success: 'He used to say, "If there's anybody thinks they're a superstar in this side, we'll see how good they are in the second eleven."'

As time went on there were players eyeing places in the England side. Jack acknowledges the place for ambition in a sportsman's career, but he was always wary of any obsession with life on the international scene that might be to the detriment of team spirit in the county dressing room. With his two overseas stars, Clive Lloyd and Farokh Engineer, he had no such concerns. Both were players who forgot any personal ambitions in pursuit of the team goal. Jack Simmons endorses this: 'Two great players who played purely for the side. Over 15 years I reckon Clive would have scored another 20 hundreds if he had played for Clive Lloyd rather than for the team.'

Jack refused to have averages pinned up in the dressing room until the end of the season, and when one of his players used an early Sunday league match as batting practice while his team-mates sacrificed their wickets in a forlorn run chase, that player was omitted from the side. Jack himself had a high reputation as a supremely unselfish player, perhaps evidenced by the high proportion of times he was dismissed caught (67%) – forcing the pace – in first-class matches. He expected no less from those who played in his team.

Universally respected at Old Trafford, the man himself is inseparable from his religious beliefs; but these take the form not of maintaining that he is in some way 'better' than his fellow men, nor that he has a faith that he must obsessively share with all but that he has a mission to help others. Asked to define his brand of Methodism, his response is: 'Friendship and fellowship, community living, bonding together, helping people less fortunate than yourself.' It is easy to see how such values translate into the cause of a team and leading that team. 'Helping young cricketers and watching them progress, I take a delight in that. If I can help somebody or suggest something to them and it works out for them – that's where I get my kicks from.'

'I've been in a position where I've been able to give people the chance to succeed or fail. I've been able to pick teams or bring people onto the staff, and it's a privileged position to give people a chance with the bat or ball. If you stick someone way down the order or never give them a decent bowl, what's the good of that? I always liked to think of myself as a chance maker.'

The concept that advice should pass only in one direction was not the Jack Bond philosophy. 'Jack never made a move without consulting me,' says Farokh Engineer. 'I knew the conditions and I could see how people were bowling better than anyone else.' Sometimes it would be little more than a nod and field adjustments would be made. 'We had a very good rapport and it was a tremendous feeling when we tried a change and it came off.'

The notion that junior players should be kept in their place was anathema to Jack. 'You never stop listening to anybody. It can be the youngest lad in the dressing room. You can be captain and suddenly he's said something and you think, yes that's right. You should never stop listening to anybody – I don't care who they are or how little they've played.' Where uncapped players, confined to their downstairs quarters, had once knocked timidly on the senior dressing-room door, now they were re-housed upstairs in what had been the opposition's room with visiting teams moved downstairs.

'There was great humour and practical jokes,' says Farokh Engineer. 'We all enjoyed each other's company.' This strong bonding helped give the side its identity in the field, enhanced by the importance Jack always gave to this side of the game. 'I've always enjoyed fielding. I couldn't understand why anybody else couldn't enjoy it. You spend more time in a cricket match in the field than you do batting. I know for a fact that I was often in the Lancashire side because I was a better fielder than somebody else.' Encouraging his players to dive for the ball, not common practice at the time, he stressed that one run saved per man was ten fewer to chase. Barry Wood, betraying his Yorkshire origins, was an initial sceptic. 'Who is going to be cleaning all these grass stains off our flannels?' Jack Simmons remembers him asking. Jack Bond's response was to find a sponsor, Brian Melville, an avid Lancashire supporter, who took on responsibility for the cleaning of the team's flannels and shirts. For many years he was there after each match to collect all the whites and he would return them a couple of days later to the dressing room, neatly pressed and on hangers.

Simmons pays tribute to Jack as 'the best man manager I ever played for' and he gives an example from a match against Kent: 'He tried Lever, Shuttleworth, Wood, Hughes and some of them had bowled twice, once at each end, and I thought, "Is he trying to get me out of the side?" A partnership had gone on with Denness and Knott and, all of a sudden, Jack just came over and he said, "Look, Jack, I've waited this long. I know you can get these two out, so go and do it." And I did! And we won the game. It was just how he said it. I was waiting – why haven't I had a go before? But before I could even open my mouth, he said, "I've saved you for this time so you can get these two out."'

Peter Lever recalls another instance of Jack's clever motivation of his bowlers. Ken Shuttleworth, opening with Higgs, was having an off day with his line and length. 'After about three overs Bondy said, "Pete, come and show this young man how to bowl." I bowled about five overs and rolled a couple over. They were 50-odd for four or five. Jack said, "Hang on a minute, Pete. Shutt, here's the ball – that's how to bowl!"' Lever, never an easy man from whom to take the ball, retired with his self-esteem boosted while his close mate Shuttleworth had had his confidence restored.

A Jack Bond team was always a disciplined side, but it was achieved with a light touch. Jack has few recollections of imposing curfews and petty rules. His philosophy was to trust his players. 'It didn't bother me how they enjoyed themselves so long as they didn't bring the club into disrepute and if they were always fit for the next day's play. We had a few rows and we had laying down the law, but that was kept to a minimum. Sometimes it would be me taking somebody to one side and letting them know how I felt and what was expected of them.'

He relates just one occasion when he had to take stronger action. 'I did once get hold of one of the senior players and I told him that we were going to have a team meeting and, for the benefit of everybody, I was going to tell him what I thought to his face. But I warned him first that I was going to do it, rather than blurting it out. It did give him time to think, and I think it was appreciated that it was done that way rather than have a big shouting match at a team meeting in front of everybody else.'

'It was the way he held the team together,' says Farokh Engineer. 'Yes, he was certainly the best captain I played under.'

Chapter Twelve
'Nobody ever locked their doors'

The idea that Jack should take up a coaching position at Old Trafford had long been in the minds of those charged with running Lancashire's cricket and, with the retirement of Buddy Oldfield, it was decided that he should be appointed coach with John Savage as his assistant. It was not quite the arrangement that Jack would have wished. His preference was for an umbrella role allowing him to retain an interest in the first-class game, but he agreed to become joint coach with Savage. During that summer he played in most of the second-team matches under the captaincy of Eddie Slinger, while taking full command for Lancashire's Under-25 games.

'It didn't work out,' he now admits, and an arrangement that had been expected to last for at least three years came to an end after only one, with Jack disenchanted to learn later that his name had been canvassed as a Test selector that summer, but that Lancashire had not been prepared to propose him. 'They said no, he's got enough on his plate. It didn't get through the committee by one vote.'

In a varied career that would never venture far from cricket for the rest of his working life and beyond, the next summer saw Jack back as a first-class player, moving from his beloved Old Trafford to Nottinghamshire. 'I'd become friendly with Jack Baddiley and John Heatley at Trent Bridge, and I'd played against Jack when I'd been in the second team and he'd been the Notts captain. He asked me to go there as cricket manager and to captain the side.'

For six years Nottinghamshire had been captained by Garfield Sobers. He had immediately revived the fortunes of a club that had taken the wooden spoon for two of the three seasons prior to his arrival, but by 1974 the lower reaches of the table were beckoning once more, in what was to be Sobers' last summer. Notts had seen a formula that had worked at Old Trafford and hoped that it might work for them, but even the best of captains have sell-by dates and

Jack had acknowledged his two years earlier. Could he once more crank up and revitalise a side in the doldrums?

Jack brought some fresh ideas to Trent Bridge. He converted opening batsman Pasty Harris into a wicket-keeper, giving the side the balance that the recruitment of Engineer had done at Old Trafford, and he brought in Harry Latchman, another former Middlesex player, as a leg-spinner. But Jack contributed little with the bat and he found it an uphill task to motivate a more mature team. 'I had gone from a county that was bubbling and bouncing to one where there was a lot of apathy, even in the crowd.'

Though Sobers was past his best, he and Harris made good runs, but there was a lack of penetration in the attack. Off-spinner Bob White, who topped the averages, looks back on a happy year with Jack in charge: 'I enjoyed playing with him. I was very impressed with his tactical know-how. He had fantastic insight into the game. Man management was his forte, and he had a wonderful sense of humour.'

Jack's humour was often needed that summer. Fifteenth place in the Championship, with just one victory against nine defeats, was a disappointment, and it was not a happier story in the John Player League, where Notts propped up the table. 'It didn't work out as I would have liked,' he now reflects rather sadly.

Before too long the county's fortunes would be restored – Notts won the Championship in 1981 – and for this Jack may take some of the credit. It was on his recommendation that Notts signed the South African Clive Rice, soon to be one of the most successful all-rounders in the county game. The young Rice had played three matches for the second team at Lancashire and Jack saw him as the ideal replacement for Sobers.

Jack remembers returning to Trent Bridge after the crucial meeting with Rice at Eastbourne to discover that the cash-strapped county wanted to reduce the playing staff to just 14 and bring in league players to fulfil second-team commitments. With so few full-time professionals, Jack felt he would have a staff too small for him to work with, so he enquired how many more players the county might be able to sign if he was released. He was told that his salary would cover two. 'I said, "Sign two more players and I'll go." And that was the end of that.'

Among the compensations for Jack in this unfulfilling interlude had been his ability to join the Test selection panel, a job for which his regular involvement on the field well equipped him. He served under the chairmanship of Alec Bedser, with Brian Taylor and Ossie Wheatley as his fellow selectors, in a summer in which Mike Denness led England to series wins against India and Pakistan. There was a first cap for David Lloyd in the second Test of the summer and a highlight of the annihilation of India and their vaunted spin attack was his double century in the next match at Edgbaston. The series against Pakistan hinged on ruthless exploitation of a rain-affected pitch at Lord's by Derek Underwood, but the limitations of the England attack were exposed in a high-scoring draw at The Oval, as the batsmen's frailties would be the following winter when confronted by the pace of Dennis Lillee and Jeff Thomson.

Jack had only the briefest taste of life as a selector, and he was not around to advise on the repair work required when the battered touring party returned home, for an advertisement in *The Cricketer* was to lead his life in an unexpected direction. King William's College on the Isle of Man sought a cricket coach and Jack's application brought a swift response. Principal of a school that was founded in 1833 was Geoffrey Rees-Jones, scorer of two famous tries in Wales' defeat of the 1936 All Blacks, and the Vice-Principal was C.I.M.Jones, one-time captain of the Great Britain hockey team and a man who had played two first-class cricket matches for Cambridge. Together they persuaded Jack to uproot and move to the island, a special carrot being that Wesley could finish his secondary education at the College.

Ian Jones, known universally as CIM, pronounced in the manner of Kipling, well remembers the happy outcome of that first meeting. 'Jack's impact was immediate. He had a marvellous way with people and he was involved with everything right from the start. I was also coaching the College hockey eleven and organised a number of scratch teams to play against the school teams and other Island teams. Jack had not played hockey since his National Service, but he was soon an integral and above all an enthusiastic member of the team. He also played Isle of Man table tennis, so was well known and accepted on the Island before the cricket season even started.'

'Together we ran the College eleven. Our first match was away at Merchant Taylor's Crosby, whom we had not beaten for some time.

We managed to bowl them out and at tea our openers were still there. On resumption Jack and I walked round the boundary and eventually I said to him, "Well, Jack, what did you tell them?" "Oh," he said, "I thought you were doing that!" We both laughed and wondered how on earth, from where we were now, we could get instructions out to our two batsmen. Fortunately our openers needed no advice and we won the match.'

King William's College at Castletown, Isle of Man.

'A few days later we found ourselves travelling together as a staff team to take on a remote village in the middle of the island. We arrived first – there was no sign of a wicket despite the local parson telling us he had prepared it and, rather than playing, he would be umpiring. It was the only match I have played in when I have seen an umpire signal six leg byes – in fact the ball had parted the scorer's hair in the shed which acted as the pavilion. When Jack went out to bat there was another first – a six hit off the gloves, with a triumphant Jack flexing his right arm muscle and expressing his delight.

'Later that summer I found myself on a hat trick bowling very experimental leg breaks. I took my courage in both hands and threw up a third leg break and there was Jack flying through the air as he had done years before to win a Gillette final to give me the one and only hat trick of my career. "I could not drop that one," he said.'

'I can see Jack taking our bowlers out on the square after matches to show them where they should have been pitching the ball and where they should have placed their fields and how the Eleven should have functioned more effectively as a team in the field. I played a lot of cricket that summer with Jack. It was always great fun.'

C.I.M.Jones moved on after this first year, in which he and Jack had combined to mould an unbeaten cricket team, to become headmaster of Bedford School. He would dearly have loved to take Jack with him, but a minor obstacle was that the resident coach, Bob Caple, once of Hampshire, had claimed CIM's wicket for a duck in one of his two forays into the first-class game – and he had no wish to seem vindictive after the passing of the years!

For Jack, his five years at King William's was a period of supreme fulfilment. The College, at that time only for boys but now co-educational, is situated at Castletown in the south of the island. Just minutes from an airport with a regular service to Heathrow, it provides easy access for pupils from across the world. 'We had Arabian princes and people like that,' Jack remembers. The College provided the family with comfortable accommodation looking westward over the sea, and Jack's mother, for the first time in her life, boarded a plane to join them in their new home. 'She used to do her ironing looking at the waves coming in. She said, "I never thought I'd end up like this!"'

It was a happy and carefree time. 'It was like going back thirty years. It was community living. Nobody ever locked their doors and things like that. We were just sort of one big family.' Jack and Florence threw themselves into the life of the island. Jack took part in amateur dramatics and well remembers being roped in by Unity Rees-Jones, the Principal's wife, as a fairy in her production of Cinderella at the Gaiety Theatre in Douglas. 'She played the fairy godmother and she was in charge of about ten fairies, all fellows. I had to appear from the back of the theatre and walk all the way to the stage and make an introductory speech and then we started the show. I was dressed in a tutu and I wore big cricket boots and carried a wand.'

Jack took part in a wide range of sports and, in playing cricket, table tennis and hockey for the Isle of Man, he now relishes the quaint notion that he quickly became a triple 'international'. 'All cricketers should have a go at hockey,' he says. 'Because it makes you play straight when you've only a stick to defend yourself. To have someone knocking a ball at you from two or three yards away, it makes you dance a bit. You have to be quick on your feet.'

Hockey was a game at which both Wesley and Stephanie excelled and there were some mixed matches in which all three Bonds could take part together. While Wesley made the most of his time at the College in the classroom and on the playing field, Stephanie worked in the x-ray department of Martin-Baker, pioneers in the manufacture of ejection seats for military jet aircraft. Meeting her future husband, Lawrence Jenkins from the Wirral, on the Island, she was married in the College chapel.

In his role as groundsman Jack worked in tandem in his first year with Syd Copley, the College's former professional. Copley had played just one first-class match for Nottinghamshire, but his place in cricket folklore was secured when, as twelfth man in the Trent Bridge Test of 1930, he held a spectacular catch at mid on to dismiss Stan McCabe. Jack and his assistants had 35 acres of playing fields, three cricket squares and ten grass nets to tend, but it was for his influence on the boys that he will be remembered. 'No-one should underestimate the enormous impact he made at King William's as a coach and above all as a man,' says C.I.M.Jones.

The pace and pleasures of life in the Isle of Man might have ensnared Jack for the rest of his days, but first-class cricket retained its own magnetic attraction for him, and the news that Lancashire were once more seemingly tethered to the lower reaches of the table meant that there was a job to be done on the mainland. And, as fate would have it, a man whose finger was now on the pulse of affairs at Old Trafford had come to live on the island, Bob Bennett. Could Jack be persuaded to return to his old hunting grounds as manager?

'When somebody suddenly asks you to put your head in a noose you have to think very carefully about it,' Jack was quoted as saying at the time. He had no illusions that the job would be an easy one. 'But the fingers have been itching since I was approached about the job,' he confessed in the same press interview after his appointment was announced towards the end of the 1979 season.

'The pace and pleasures of life.'
Jack taking part in the World Tin Bath Championship,
in Castletown Harbour in 1976.

Table tennis team, Isle of Man style:
Jack with two College boys and the village postman.

Chapter Thirteen
'I don't mean me – I mean thee!'

The strength of Jack's captaincy had been a united team committed to following his lead. 'Most of them had nowhere else to turn,' he had said. But could it ever be the same as a manager? A few other counties had appointed managers – Les Ames at Kent and, more recently, Ray Illingworth at Yorkshire – but for most it was still an alien idea, and a brief period with Cyril Washbrook as Lancashire's manager in the mid-sixties had not brought success.

The golden days of Jack Bond had not been sustained. Under David Lloyd there had been three more Lord's finals, but only one victory. John Player performances had declined and a promising fourth place in the Championship in 1975 was followed by two wretched years when Lancashire ended just one place from the bottom of the table. In 1978 Frank Hayes had taken over, but the county still clung to a double-digit position in the Championship, with no one-day triumphs to offer compensation.

Aware that things could not drift on, Chairman Cedric Rhoades saw the appointment of a manager as the way the game had to go. 'No matter how strong a captain may be, and how devoted he is to the job, the days have gone when he can shoulder the whole of the burden.' The terms of the job were made plain: 'Jack Bond is coming back to take absolute control of the players and the coaching staff. His title of cricket manager means he will be responsible to the club's general committee through me.'

There was a groundswell of support for Jack. Frank Hayes was quoted as seeing Jack as 'the right man for the job', though he added more ominously that he was 'perhaps, the only man who could do it.' Stressing that supporters should not be expecting miracles, Jack set to work. There followed seven years during which the highest championship place was twelfth, most seasons saw Lancashire below half-way in the John Player and winning the Benson and Hedges in 1984 was the only knockout success.

What went wrong? Players who remember both periods admit that the side of the early 1970s, with its high quotient of international players, was vastly superior to the teams put out at the start of the next decade. By the time Jack returned, Lever and Engineer had both retired, the Indian to be replaced by a string of less capable keeper-batsmen, Shuttleworth had moved to Leicestershire and faded out of the game and Wood had switched to Derbyshire, while Pilling's efforts were now directed towards helping the second team. David Lloyd soldiered on till the end of 1982, while Hayes batted well in 1980, but soon became a victim of injury and was a waning talent by the time of his retirement in 1983.

Jack Simmons remained, but age was not his ally, while David Hughes declined as a wicket-taking bowler, though his batting developed. These two, with Clive Lloyd, who returned to Lancashire after missing the 1980 season to captain the West Indian tourists, were the last of those who had been part of the earlier triumphs. Inevitably there were promising new players who burst upon the scene, often to a fanfare of optimistic publicity. But Jack goes through the list of the men who never really made it. For one it was a lack of passion for the game, with a couple of others nerves proved too inhibiting, for another alcohol was his secret undoing, while there were those who simply lacked fight when the chips were down. Only two new players, Graeme Fowler and Paul Allott, made it into the Test side.

There might have been one more had the South African-born Neil Radford been more inclined to listen to advice. Jack grew tired of stressing to him the importance of getting close to the stumps. 'It was only after he had gone to Worcestershire that he must have listened to someone.' In 1985, his first season with his new county, Radford was the country's leading wicket-taker and went on to win three Test caps.

At no time did Lancashire have a truly settled side. So playing for a place once again became a priority in a squad already less cohesive for having more disparate ages. From his time as captain Jack had seen the price that can be paid when players are called up for Test cricket. Now the problem raised its head again: 'All they could talk about was England – even when they came back to play games for us. "They do it this way with England, they do it that way". They're shoving that down everybody's throat, which isn't good for morale in the dressing room.'

123

In 1983 Peter Lever joined as first-team coach. He had admired Jack's captaincy and, for all his Yorkshire stubbornness, he had fitted into the team as a player; but, in their different roles, it wasn't so easy and it was soon less certain in the dressing room who was running the show – manager, coach or captain. 'It never works when there's two people in charge,' one former player comments, with the question of the person to whom the players reported further confused by trying to guess who might be in favour with the committee. Where the successful team that Jack had captained had all enjoyed each other's company, now cliques formed. The culture of fear, so prevalent in the Old Trafford of the 1960s, returned, and it was nurtured by lack of success.

Cedric Rhoades had done much to help put Lancashire back on the road, but he was under growing pressure from lack of success. 'At first he was fighting for the players,' says Peter Lever, 'but then his own importance overtook his initial aims.' Rhoades had championed Jack's return, and he had spoken of his manager having unfettered control of team matters, but by the start of 1986 ten seasons had passed with Lancashire no higher than twelfth in the championship table.

Changes of captain continued. After the 1980 season, the third for Frank Hayes, Clive Lloyd was appointed. A highly successful captain of an exceptional Test side, Lloyd himself has always felt that he might have done better for his adopted county had he been installed earlier. Now he had poor quality bricks with which to build and, though still a fine batsman, he was not quite the force he had been, while trouble with his back had ended his days as an inspirational fielder in the covers and he had to be content to direct affairs from slip.

With Lloyd again leading the touring team in 1984, a new skipper was required and Jack promoted John Abrahams. After waiting ten years to win his county cap, Abrahams had enjoyed two decent seasons with the bat and had personal qualities that appealed to Jack. 'John had had to fight his way through the game like I had to.' The appointment was not universally welcomed among the players and there were doubters on the committee. Nevertheless Jack felt his chosen man did a decent job in his first year, the highlight of which was winning the Benson and Hedges Cup, in which Peter May's surprise choice as the final's Man of the Match was the Lancashire skipper. Abrahams had made a duck, but won the award for his captaincy and fielding.

The coaches' lot.
Jack, with John Savage, anxiously awaiting the outcome of the Benson and Hedges final at Lord's, July 1984. Lancashire won by six wickets.

The following year, with Clive Lloyd back but now playing fewer matches to accommodate fast bowler Patrick Patterson as the only permitted overseas player, Abrahams remained in charge. Fourteenth in the Championship, with nothing to show for their efforts in the one-day game, meant that there was the inevitable call for change, while six years of disappointment meant that Jack's job was on the line.

For Jack and Florence, cricket now assumed its rightful perspective as they learned, in January of that year, of the death of their son Wesley in a motoring accident. Jack had been coaching with John Savage in the indoor school when Wesley and a fellow member of Disley Hockey Club, Michael Jordan, had been making use of the Old Trafford gym. The two young men had left and returned to Michael's home, later popping out in the car for a take-away meal. On their return there was a fatal collision with a late-night bus.

The first that Jack and Florence knew of the tragedy was in the early hours of 22 January, when a policeman knocked on the door of the Jodrell Arms, the pub in Whaley Bridge where all the family had lived after their return from the Isle of Man. Someone from that address, they learned, had been involved in a fatal accident. Only then did they discover that Wesley had not returned home. Stephanie's husband Lawrence went down to identify the body and confirmed their worst fears.

Wesley was just 25 and had embarked on a career in banking before switching to the wine and spirits trade. A memorial stone stands at the Disley Club, ensuring that their two young members will not be forgotten. 'They say time's a healer, but it isn't really,' Jack says. 'It is still with me all the time. Probably not as severe and as heart-rending, but it's still there.' His Christian faith was tested, but it helped to sustain him. 'Without a faith, I doubt if we'd have got through that situation even though we didn't think it should have happened. And we had a lot of help – that's what Methodism is all about.'

A shadow was cast over what was to be Jack's last season as manager. It had not begun propitiously with the committee's choice of Clive Lloyd to resume the captaincy of the club. Jack's own preference would have been to bring in an outsider, a move alien to his traditional instincts. He had suggested that approaches might be made to two former England players, Chris Tavaré, ousted from the captaincy at Kent, or Vic Marks, blocked by Peter Roebuck from taking over at Somerset.

Jack retained the highest regard for Clive Lloyd as a player and a man, but he foresaw the absurdity of a captain sitting out most matches if the county wished to make use of the Caribbean pace of Patterson. However, Lloyd was the committee's choice and he had to live with it, notwithstanding the chairman's initial assertion that, as manager, he would 'take absolute control'. An assurance had been given to the committee by Lloyd that he would be around the dressing room even if he was not playing in a match. Across the championship season the captain played in just six matches – he had made only four appearances the previous year, while the team was now led, at different times, by Simmons, the appointed vice-captain, although he was no longer a cast-iron choice for the three-day side, Abrahams and Fowler. A side already looking in three directions for a lead could now have four people whose views might count. It was the recipe for disaster that Jack had foreseen.

Fifteenth place in the Championship, twelfth equal in the John Player and failure to progress beyond the group stage in the Benson and Hedges were the components of another disappointing season, leavened only by reaching the final of what was now styled the NatWest Trophy. This match, against Sussex, was notable for an emotional farewell to Lord's from Clive Lloyd, playing at the expense of Patterson's fire power. The genial giant could not live up to supporters' hopes, departing lbw to his fourth ball. Lancashire posted 242 for eight, with a young Neil Fairbrother making 63. It was not enough to prevent a Sussex victory by seven wickets with ten balls to spare.

Two days later Jack was sacked, a decision taken by five votes to four by a committee that also decided to dispense with the services of the coach. Even looking back to this lowest hour in his time with Lancashire, Jack's humour remains intact, the story of his dismissal featuring in his after dinner speeches. 'Cedric was at one end of this great long table and I'm at the other end of it. Cedric said, "I'm sorry, I think it's time to call it a day." And I said, "I don't really think so, chairman. I think you're doing a grand job." He said, "No, not me, I mean thee!"'

There was to be a more acrimonious sequel when the Annual General Meeting came round in December. A member, Ken Thomas, paid tribute to Clive Lloyd as a player, but questioned the wisdom of his appointment as captain. Was this, he enquired, a decision taken on the recommendation of the manager? Informed that all such appointments were taken by recommendation, Thomas repeated his question to which, as recorded in the minutes, 'the Chairman replied in the affirmative.'

Jack, who attended the meeting as an ordinary member, held his tongue. But he was incensed and was soon putting the record straight. After making the recommendation that the club should seek an outsider, he and Peter Lever had left the room. The committee then decided against such an appointment. 'At no stage did they come back and ask us to recommend someone from within the club,' he informed the media. 'I thought at the time that it would cost me my job –and it did.'

There was a hostile response to Rhoades' misleading of the members, with Frank Hayes calling for a Special General Meeting. Jack simply wished the truth to be known, but Rhoades took the message and quickly resigned. The appointment as the new captain of David Hughes, who had been working with the second team in 1986, was a decision which Jack would have endorsed. Hughes at last led the county to happier times as new players first identified in Jack's time – Fairbrother, Atherton, Watkinson and Hegg – came to fruition, soon to be joined by Wasim Akram as an inspired overseas signing.

Lt-Gen Sir James Wilson, football correspondent of the Sunday Times, hosting a group of northern sporting personalities and their wives at an Army headquarters in Preston.
Also in the picture: Joe Mercer, Tom Finney, Sir Matt Busby and Bobby Charlton.

Chapter Fourteen
'He'll cook the bacon sandwiches'

Jack's second departure from Old Trafford meant that he was able to devote more time to the Jodrell Arms. On their return from the Isle of Man, he and Florence had looked for a business that they could run in partnership with Lawrence and Stephanie. The view across the Irish Sea had inspired thoughts of a boarding house at Blackpool, but they had taken a tenancy of the small hotel, at Whaley Bridge in Derbyshire, because it was a more convenient base for working at Old Trafford. With eleven bedrooms and a kitchen and bar to run, Florence and the other members of the family were always busily employed, and for a while Jack was now able to give them more assistance, particularly enjoying the chance to resume the banter across the bar that had always been a feature of life in the fish-and-chip shop.

He spent the summer of 1987 playing cricket for Whaley Bridge in the Derbyshire and Cheshire League. Now 55, he found that table tennis and fell walking in the winter kept him fit, and he was still able to make a decent number of runs for the club. There was one century at Hawk Green, and he held some good slip catches. But he found the first-class game still beckoning.

Disinclined to try for another coaching post, he applied to join the umpires' list. He trained up during the winter, though other commitments prevented him from completing his course. He was nevertheless accepted for the reserve list but, before the season started, David Lloyd withdrew from the first-class panel to take up a position as a commentator with Sky Television, and Jack received a call from Lord's to say that he was to be promoted into the vacancy.

His first match was at Oxford, where he stood in The Parks with Nigel Plews, appointed to the Test match panel for the first time that summer. So began ten years travelling the county circuit, punctuated by just two appointments as third umpire in Test matches in 1993, in the days shortly before the duties extended to watching a television monitor. 'You were just a ball carrier. The only time you would get on was if someone was taken ill.'

For Jack it was another happy period of his life. He enjoyed the chance to watch good players from 'the best seat in the house', though he had to train himself to avoid becoming too absorbed in the ebbs and flows of the game to the detriment of the job he was supposed to be doing. He reflects on the changes he has seen that made the job less convivial than it had once been. In his playing days, when there had been no television in hotel rooms, he had been used to finding the likes of Charlie Elliott, Jack Crapp, Bill Copson and Ron Aspinall in the bar at the team's hotel. 'They were happy to be among cricketers.' In the modern game there is less fraternising, and Jack's own philosophy is that 'it's a dangerous practice, to be having a drink with somebody one night and giving him out first ball next morning.'

With less mixing with the players at close of play, an umpire looks to his colleague for companionship. 'The first thing you look at when you get your fixtures is not who the match is against but who you are standing with.' A potentially lonely life, travelling alone up the motorways, is eased by reuniting with a good friend at the ground. 'You're glad to be standing with someone like Jack with his marvellous sense of humour,' says Bob White, just as Jack himself would relish three days with 'Knocker' and many others on the list. Sometimes his fellow umpire lived close enough to get home for the night, and Jack then preferred to avoid larger hotels in favour of the family atmosphere of a farm or bed-and-breakfast.

On the field Jack learned to be philosophical. 'You've got to get it out of your head that you are going to get everything right,' he says. Players' expressions, not necessarily in open dissent, can make an umpire realise that he has made a wrong decision. 'And there's nothing worse than on the first morning of a three-day game when you get something wrong and you realise quite quickly that you got it wrong, and you think there's another three days to go. It can play on your mind.'

Players do not always realise, Jack feels, that when conditions are difficult for batting with the ball seaming around, they are also difficult for umpiring. But some of the umpires do! 'There's always one end that's the business end, and there's one or two senior umpires who are quite cute. They know which end there's a gale blowing, so they'll go and stand at the other end! Because the fast bowler will be running in with the wind behind him and it'll be difficult down that end.'

Jack was brought up in an age when batsmen took much of the pressure off the umpire. 'If you hit it, you walk,' had been the way Stan Worthington had schooled the young professionals. 'You could count the people on one hand in English cricket who didn't walk,' says Jack. And a fielder's word on a catch was accepted. From Jack's time at Old Trafford in the 1980s, Steve O'Shaughnessy, now himself an umpire, learned that this was still the ethos when his manager sent him to apologise to Arthur Jepson after he had made a gesture to show that a ball had brushed his shoulder not his bat. By the 1990s it had all changed. Few players were any longer helping the umpires with their decisions, and Jack was disappointed to find that some of those with whom he had played were tempted to cheat as their careers threatened to be drawing to a close. Now the game he watches has more aggravation, and for this, he blames the captains. 'I don't think they are doing their job on the field sometimes.'

John Higson, chairman of Gloucestershire, toasts Barry Meyer and Jack on their retirement from the first-class umpires panel in 1997.

Jack's involvement in umpiring brought him an invitation to travel to Argentina as assistant manager of an MCC party captained by the Sussex and England batsman Paul Parker and managed by John Jameson, Assistant Secretary (Cricket) at Lord's. It was a time of some diplomatic sensitivity as the tour, in March 1990, was the first of its kind since the Falklands War.

On earlier tours to the country, MCC had been opposed principally by expatriates, but the sides they now played were made up mostly of locally born-and-bred players, and Jack was relieved to find that the hostilities of eight years earlier never figured in conversations. Ten one-day matches were played, with MCC's only loss helped by six lbw decisions from their own umpire. 'They were mostly on the front foot,' Jack now recalls. 'All these club players thought they could just push forward and they'd be safe. But they soon learned that they couldn't!'

Five years earlier, another overseas trip had taken Jack to India. This time he went, accompanied by Florence, as assistant manager on a Christians in Sport tour. Arranged and led by the Reverend Andrew Wingfield-Digby, a man who was later to enjoy a brief spell as chaplain to the England team, the party included prominent county cricketers such as Vic Marks, Roger Knight, Simon Hughes and Graham Cowdrey. Jack's principal on-field role was as umpire, though he played in one of the games.

The timing of the tour is etched in his mind as he and Florence had left with Stephanie about to give birth to her second child. At a time when overseas calls had still to be booked in advance, Jack and Florence emerged from a laying-on of hands and healing service in one of the cathedrals in Madras eager for news of their daughter. But so bad was the Madras pollution that, when they were finally connected to the Jodrell Arms, they found that they had both lost their voices and were unable to speak to Lawrence, leading Jack to quip that two of the people at the healing service must have gone out of the cathedral with Lancashire accents!

The last two decades have seen an explosion in the market for winter tours following the fortunes of the England side abroad. Sometimes as many as two dozen different companies organise parties, and a leader in the field is ITC, for whom Jack is one of their most regular and popular 'cricket personalities'. Jack Simmons, who recommended his former captain for the job, notes how some companies like to find recently retired Test stars, but he says that clients of ITC ring up and say, 'Which tour is Jack Bond taking? Whichever he's taking, we'll go on it.'

To Jack, who is always accompanied by Florence, it is more than just a chance to follow the sun. Hosting a tour is an extension of all that he has most valued in life; meeting people from all walks of life, having a chance to help them and talking endlessly about the game of cricket. And the cricketing nuts whose savings go on these tours learn from the expertise of one who has thought deeply about the game: 'I can't understand why Monty's bowling from this end with the breeze. And why hasn't he got a slip?'

There have been moments of triumph for England, but many days of disappointment when Jack's lifetime fondness for the rousing music of brass bands and his knowledge of hymns – 'I know my hymns better than I know my bible' – come to the rescue. 'I'll say, "Now look, England have had a bad day yesterday, so this morning I think we'd better sing a hymn." And I'll sing a sportsman's hymn like "Guide me, O thou great Jehovah". It's surprising the number of people that join in.' 'Bread of Heaven', 'Land of my Fathers,' 'In the bleak midwinter' – to remember snow-encased Britain in the early days of 2010 – and such ballads as 'I'll take you home again, Kathleen' ring out in the coach. And Jack's favourite party pieces, the Stanley Holloway monologues – 'yon lion's ate Albert' and 'Sam, Sam, pick up thy musket' – add to the conviviality as sorrows are drowned in the local beverage and the holiday spirit is restored.

Jack looks back on a life with few regrets apart from the weeks away from his family that is the lot of most leading sportsmen. He remains loyal to his roots. Now living in Bury, he and Florence still make the 35-minute drive on a Sunday to worship at the Methodist church almost opposite the old fish-and-chip shop in Little Hulton, where their teenage romance began and where they were married. The family remains closely knit. Stephanie, who lives nearby, is mother to three grandchildren for Jack and Florence.

The eldest, Natalie, lives in Redditch with Steve, her husband from a holiday romance, and young Grace, a first great-grandchild for Jack and Florence. Natalie has worked for the past eleven years as sales and marketing coordinator for Bobst, the packaging machinery manufacturer. Her younger sister, Kate, worked in the publicity department of the *Bolton Evening News* and *Bury Times* before moving on to take an account management job with North West Design Studios in Atherton. 'She's doing very well,' Jack says with pride. And he is especially touched that his youngest grandchild, 17-year-old Wesley, should have been named after an uncle he was so sadly deprived of knowing.

Worsley Road North Methodist Church in early 2010.

Four generations of Bonds.
From left: Jack, Natalie, Florence, Stephanie (holding Grace) and Kate.

Has Jack really retired from cricket? He loves to joke that he has been sacked twice by Lancashire, but it hasn't stopped him risking his neck by returning to Old Trafford a third time. 'He just loves the place,' says Jack Simmons, Lancashire's chairman for ten years, who has been able to see his former captain – and a man elected a vice-president of the club in 1996 – patiently preparing pitches for the nets on the last remaining grass of what was once a full practice ground. If the weather is right and there is a job to be done, Jack will be there two or three days a week, scarifying, mowing and rolling the surface on which the hopefuls of tomorrow can hone their skills.

For a man from the era before mega-benefits who is always generous to a fault – 'Jack would still be buying a round of drinks if it was his last fiver,' says Jack Simmons – the work brings in useful pin money. But let Chief Executive, Jim Cumbes, the man who has it in his power to complete the hat trick of dismissals, have the final word: 'He's a lovely man, Jack. Still doing a useful job, but I think the ground staff are more interested in the fact that he'll cook the bacon sandwiches in the morning.'

Jack's grandchildren Kate and Wesley.

Acknowledgements and Bibliography

A book of this kind, in which a living cricketer has shared his memories, must always owe most to its subject. To have worked with Jack Bond has been a very special privilege.

My thanks are due to all who have given me time, whether face-to-face, on the telephone or by letter or e-mail to share recollections of Jack. I should especially mention Bob Barber, Jim Cumbes, Farokh Engineer, C.I.M.Jones, Peter Lever, Clive Lloyd, Frank Parr, Jack Simmons, Roy Tattersall, Brigadier Harry Thompson and Bob White. I am also grateful to Trevor Pledger for unearthing full details of Jack's playing record at Bolton School.

I have made regular use of the following reference books:

Wisden Cricketers' Almanack
Playfair Cricket Annual
Benny Green (ed), *The Wisden Book of Obituaries*, Macdonald Queen Anne Press, 1986
Philip Bailey, Philip Thorn and Peter Wynne-Thomas, *Who's Who of Cricketers* (Second Edition), Hamlyn Books, 1993
E.W.Swanton and George Plumptre (eds), *Barclays World of Cricket*, Collins, 1986

I have consulted and sometimes quoted from:

Vernon Addison and Brian Bearshaw, *Lancashire Cricket at the Top*, Stanley Paul, 1971
Brian Bearshaw, *From the Stretford End*, Partridge Press, 1990
Stephen Chalke, *At the Heart of English Cricket*, Fairfield Books, 2001
Simon Lister, *Supercat*, Fairfield Books, 2007
John Marshall, *Old Trafford*, Pelham Books, 1971
Gordon Ross, *The Gillette Cup 1963 to 1980*, Queen Anne Press, 1981

I have consulted and quoted from sundry newspapers, principally *The Times, The Guardian, The Manchester Evening News* and *The Evening Chronicle*, but also others, not always identifiable in a limited scrapbook maintained for the early years of Jack Bond's career by his wife, Florence.

I am grateful to the Reverend Malcolm Lorimer and Jim Cumbes, Chief Executive of Lancashire CCC for arranging for me to have access to the County's minute books and other archive material, including a book of cuttings on Jack Bond.

I am grateful also to my friend John Gallimore for an extended loan of a run of *Wisdens* that I borrowed 'for a few days'.

My principal source of statistics has been cricketarchive.com

Many photographs and other illustrations come from Jack Bond's family album. A number of others have been kindly supplied by the Press Association and by Keith Hayhurst from his private collection. The County Club, through the good offices of Malcolm Lorimer and Ken Grime, have also been helpful in making other photographs available. The picture of the Methodist Church at Walkden, where Jack and Florence worship, was specially taken by Ian Lord.

Especial thanks must go to my friend Stephen Chalke for kindly offering to read an early draft of the text. I have striven to incorporate many of his invaluable suggestions for improvement. I stand in awe of David Jeater, as helpful an editor as any author could hope to find, for his eagle eye and his mastery of punctuation. Philip Bailey has, as ever, provided timely statistical advice. I knew I could relax when I heard that Chris Overson and Gerald Hudd had been assigned the task of proofreading. I am yet another ACS author grateful to Peter Griffiths for his unfailing attention to detail in preparing the text for printing and for ensuring that ACS standards are maintained. To Zahra Ridge, a more recent recruit to the ACS publishing team, my thanks for a cover design that must help the book to commend itself to Lancashire supporters.

Appendix
Career Statistics

First-Class Cricket: Batting and Fielding

	M	I	NO	R	HS	Ave	100	50	Ct
1955	2	3	0	26	25	8.66	-	-	1
1957	23	32	1	608	72	19.61	-	6	24
1958	10	14	0	133	25	9.50	-	-	4
1959	18	33	6	862	101*	31.92	1	7	16
1960	18	28	3	565	105*	22.60	2	1	16
1961	35	58	11	1701	152	36.19	3	8	18
1962	36	67	8	2125	157	36.01	5	9	22
1963	11	19	1	239	38	13.27	-	-	8
1964	12	21	3	502	105*	27.88	1	1	8
1965	15	26	1	484	112*	19.36	1	1	5
1966	22	38	5	743	90	22.51	-	3	5
1967	17	27	6	649	97	30.90	-	4	13
1968	30	43	10	878	93*	26.60	-	2	13
1969	27	33	3	723	90	24.10	-	5	14
1970	25	33	9	780	89	32.50	-	5	25
1971	24	31	6	561	54*	22.44	-	1	16
1972	20	18	3	301	103*	20.06	1	-	11
1974	17	24	4	245	65*	12.25	-	1	3
Totals	**362**	**548**	**80**	**12125**	**157**	**25.90**	**14**	**54**	**222**

Notes: All Bond's first-class cricket was played in England and Wales, 344 matches for Lancashire, 17 for Nottinghamshire and one for MCC. He did not play first-class cricket in 1956 and 1973. He was dismissed 315 times caught (67%, an unusually high proportion); 98 times bowled (21%); 34 times lbw (7%); 12 times run out (3%) and nine times stumped (2%). The bowlers who took his wicket most often were G.A.R Lock (ten times), O.S.Wheatley (eight times), and D.Shackleton, D.L.Underwood, J.A.Flavell, D.J.Shepherd and M.N.S.Taylor (seven times). As a fielder he held twenty or more catches off the bowling of K.Higgs, T.Greenhough, P.Lever, D.P.Hughes and J.B.Statham.

First-Class Cricket: Bowling

	O	M	R	W	BB	Ave	5i	10m
1959	4	1	18	0	-	-	-	-
1960	3	0	17	0	-	-	-	-
1962	2.1	0	22	0	-	-	-	-
1965	1	0	3	0	-	-	-	-
1971	1	0	9	0	-	-	-	-
Totals	**11.1**	**1**	**69**	**0**	**-**	**-**	**-**	**-**

Notes: Overs were of six balls throughout Bond's career. He conceded runs at a rate of 6.17 per over. A very occasional leg-spinner, he is one of 36 cricketers, all but seven of them wicket-keepers, who have played in 350 first-class matches or more without taking a wicket.

First-Class cricket: Centuries (14)

Score	For	Opponent	Venue	Season
101*	Lancashire[2]	Nottinghamshire	Trent Bridge	1959
100*	Lancashire[1]	South Africans	Old Trafford	1960
105*	Lancashire[1]	Somerset	Old Trafford	1960
105	Lancashire[1]	Cambridge University	Fenner's	1961
106	Lancashire[1]	Sussex	Old Trafford	1961
152	Lancashire[2]	Somerset	Bath	1961
109	Lancashire[1]	Pakistanis	Old Trafford	1962
118	Lancashire[2]	Essex	Liverpool	1962
144	Lancashire[1]	Yorkshire	Headingley	1962
157	Lancashire[2]	Hampshire	Old Trafford	1962
109	Lancashire[1]	Yorkshire	Old Trafford	1962
105*	Lancashire[1]	Hampshire	Old Trafford	1964
112*	Lancashire[2]	Leicestershire	Leicester	1965
103*	Lancashire[1]	Middlesex	Lord's	1972

Notes: The index figures [1] and [2] indicate the innings in which the score was achieved. His century against Leicestershire was at Grace Road.

List A Cricket: Batting and Fielding

	M	I	NO	R	HS	Ave	100	50	Ct
1963	1	1	0	7	7	7.00	-	-	1
1964	2	2	0	33	33	16.50	-	-	-
1965	1	1	0	0	0	-	-	-	-
1966	1	1	0	29	29	29.00	-	-	-
1967	2	2	0	3	2	1.50	-	-	-
1968	1	1	0	27	27	27.00	-	-	-
1969	16	15	2	159	43	12.33	-	-	9
1970	20	13	6	150	35*	21.42	-	-	5
1971	21	15	5	115	26*	11.50	-	-	6
1972	19	12	3	96	29*	10.66	-	-	6
1974	15	11	4	79	27	11.28	-	-	4
Totals	**99**	**74**	**20**	**698**	**43**	**12.92**	**-**	**-**	**31**

Notes: All Bond's List A cricket was played in England and Wales, with 84 matches for Lancashire and 15 for Nottinghamshire. His highest score was 43 for Lancashire against Derbyshire at Old Trafford in 1969. He was dismissed 34 times caught (63%); ten times bowled (18%); seven times run out (13%) and three times lbw (5%). He did not bowl in List A cricket.

Umpiring in First-Class and List A Cricket

Jack Bond stood in 165 first-class and 178 List A matches, almost all between 1988 and 1997, with one List A match in 1998.

Sources: cricketarchive.com and *Wisden Cricketers' Almanack*.

Index

A page number in bold type indicates an illustration.